FOUNDATIONS OF CHRISTIAN BELIEF

An Introductory Course in Apologetics

Foundations of Christian Belief

An Introductory Course in Apologetics

BY

Edward V. Stanford, O.S.A.

THE NEWMAN PRESS · WESTMINSTER, MARYLAND
1962

First Published 1960
Second Printing 1961
Third Printing 1962

Imprimi potest:

JAMES A. DONELLON, O.S.A.
Prior Provincial

February 10, 1960

Nihil obstat:

JOSEPH L. SHANNON, O.S.A., S.T.D.
Censor Deputatis

Imprimatur:

†PATRICK A. O'BOYLE, D.D.
Archbishop of Washington

March 1, 1960

The *nihil obstat* and *imprimatur* are official declarations that a book or pamphlet is free of doctrinal and moral error. No implication is contained therein that those who have granted the *nihil obstat* and *imprimatur* agree with the opinions expressed.

Library of Congress Catalog Card Number: 60-10729
Printed in the United States of America

TO THE

MOST REVEREND PATRICK A. O'BOYLE, D.D.

ARCHBISHOP OF WASHINGTON

THIS BOOK IS

RESPECTFULLY AND AFFECTIONATELY

DEDICATED

Foreword

IN A COUNTRY with a pluralistic religious situation such as we have in the United States, it is especially important for our Catholic laity to have a good understanding of the reasonable foundations of Catholic belief. To be able to give reasons for the faith that is in us we must have an intellectual grasp of the teachings of our faith. That is why we hear much today about theology for the layman.

In *Foundations of Christian Belief* we have not only a fitting but the necessary preparation for such a theology. Briefly and without digressing on side issues, the author presents the full sweep of the traditional apologetic argument which leads from unbelief to the door of the Catholic Church. Moreover, the author has simplified the argument and expressed it with clarity and directness in language that can readily be understood by the average reader.

As an educator with many years of experience, Father Stanford is particularly concerned in this book with our youth —and rightly so. However, it would seem that his book fills an even wider need and should be welcomed not only by our schools, but also by parish discussion groups and by the general reading public.

PATRICK A. O'BOYLE, D.D.
Archbishop of Washington

Preface

FOUNDATIONS OF CHRISTIAN BELIEF is an introductory course for that branch of study which, traditionally, is called *apologetics.* It is intended primarily for senior high school students, although it should be useful also for junior college, for lay study groups and for all who seek an understanding of the reasonable foundations which uphold belief in God, in man's spiritual destiny, and in the one true Church established by Christ.

Catholic youth of today, like other youth, are inclined to question and to be skeptical of authority. We have no reason to think that religious faith is excluded from this questioning. Moreover, our youth are associated with non-Catholics who have less hold on the fundamentals of religion than ever before. Hence Catholic youth may be ripe for difficulties when they hear questioned for the first time truths and facts which they have perhaps always taken on faith. If one has never had an opportunity to understand the reasonable basis of faith, such doubts may lead to serious weakening or loss of faith.

The author realizes the difficulty of presenting the complete apologetic argument to those whose mental maturity may not permit them to grasp fully the logical reasoning involved. Nevertheless he believes that much is to be gained by demonstrating what secure footholds reason can give in making the ascent from the depths of unbelief to the door of the Catholic Church.

There is reason to believe that the presenting of fragments of the apologetic argument in general religion texts may be ineffective, even harmful. Therefore in this text a complete apologetic argument is presented, beginning with proofs for the existence of God and ending with the proof that the Catholic Church is the one true Church founded by Jesus Christ.

The apologetic argument is covered briefly, but completely, in chapters one to thirteen inclusive. Chapter fourteen is an argument for the divine institution of the Catholic Church drawn from an examination of her past history, present status, and certain marvelous characteristics she possesses. Chapters fifteen and sixteen treat of topics usually found as objections in an apologetics text. Chapter seventeen deals with "Appreciating the Faith" and its implications. Although this topic is clearly outside the scope of apologetics, it does have a certain appropriateness as a practical conclusion for one who is already a member of the true Church of Christ.

The text is brief and to the point so that it may be covered readily in one semester. Supplementary reading is recommended most earnestly. There is an annotated list of suggested readings from books and pamphlets at the end of each chapter and an additional list at the end of the book.

As a minimum, the reading of the Four Gospels and the Acts of the Apostles should be required. It is suggested that this reading be completed before finishing chapter eight of the text. Thereafter, whenever studying or reading any place in the text from chapters eight to fourteen, the Four Gospels should be at hand so that all quotations in the text may be checked in the context of the Gospels. Even more important, those gospel incidents cited by chapter and verse but merely alluded to in a word or phrase should be read in their entirety.

The Confraternity of Christian Doctrine version of the New Testament is recommended for use because all the gospel quotations in this text were taken therefrom.

"Review Questions" based on the text are given at the end of each chapter. An additional seventy-five "Questions for Discussion" are to be found in the Teachers' Manual. These latter questions are not based directly on the text. They are intended to expand and apply the text matter whenever students have the ability and time to deal with collateral topics.

A Glossary has been included at the end of the text. It should be referred to whenever the student finds an unfamiliar term.

EDWARD V. STANFORD, O.S.A.
St. Mary's Hall, Villanova, Pa.

Acknowledgments

THE WRITER MAKES grateful acknowledgment to the Very Reverend Joseph L. Shannon, O.S.A., S.T.D., Professor of Dogmatic Theology at Augustinian College, Washington, D.C. Father Shannon read the manuscript with painstaking care and made very helpful suggestions. The writer is also indebted to the following for helpful suggestions: Father Walter G. Rafter, O.S.A., Villanova University; Father Edward L. Daley, O.S.A., Good Counsel Novitiate; Father Donald E. Brennam, O.S.A. and Father Francis R. McDonnell, O.S.A., Austin Preparatory School; and Father John J. Hagen, O.S.A., Augustinian Academy.

The writer also wishes to express sincere thanks to the following publishers and authors who have kindly given permission to use material from their publications: The Confraternity of Christian Doctrine for permission to use the Confraternity version of the New Testament in all quotations from the Gospels; M. H. Gill and Son, Ltd., for quotations from *Apologetics and Catholic Doctrine* by the late Most Reverend Michael Sheehan, D.D.; P. J. Kenedy & Sons, for *Rebuilding a Lost Faith,* by John L. Stoddard; Sheed and Ward for *Restoration* by Ross J. S. Hoffman; The Catholic Education Press, for *Religion Outlines for Colleges, Course II,* by John M. Cooper; Professor Fred Hoyle of Cambridge University for permission to quote from his article, "When Time Begins," which appeared in the *Saturday Evening Post.*

Contents

FOUNDATIONS OF CHRISTIAN BELIEF

An Introductory Course in Apologetics

FPG photo

The *electronic microscope* pictured above is capable of producing magnifications up to 100,000 diameters. Such scientific wonders have opened up new visions in the unseen material world, bringing to light inconceivably small microorganisms which reason told man existed but which he had never been able to see. However, these microscopes have not dispensed with the necessity of taking on human faith the existence of many other things in the physical world, of which man's reason informs him but which his senses have never been able to apprehend directly.

It is only reasonable, then, for man to accept on divine faith the existence of the unseen spiritual world to which his reason bears testimony.

Chapter 1

Faith and reason

The Importance of Faith

THE MAN WHO SAYS that he will believe only what he can prove is fooling himself. Even in a human way the knowledge that we derive from our own experience is pitiably small in comparison to what we accept on the authority of others. We must have faith then. We cannot live without it even for a day. In a strict sense we can say that *faith* is believing something on the *authority* of another. If that authority resides in a human being like ourselves, we have *human faith.* If that authority is God or what God has revealed through the Church, we have *divine faith.*

We readily accept on human faith a thousand and one things, such as: the purity of our water supply, the existence of countries we have never seen, or the truth of established scientific facts we cannot prove. In accepting these matters on human faith we must admit that it is possible for our human authorities to be themselves deceived or to deceive us. However, this causes us little real concern because we simply have to take that chance. We are not in a position to prove everything for ourselves.

But when we make use of divine faith to know truths in the supernatural order, we have no need for reservations. Once we know that God has revealed a certain truth, we have the strongest possible reasons for believing in it, since God cannot deceive us or be Himself deceived. Consequently, in the familiar prayer, *An Act of Faith,* we say: "My God, I firmly believe all the sacred truths which the Holy Catholic Church believes and teaches because Thou hast revealed them, who canst neither deceive nor be deceived." Our reasons for divine faith are the strongest possible reasons, far stronger than our reasons for human faith.

Not only is the belief founded on divine faith stronger, but it is also more blessed. A single gospel incident makes this abundantly clear. Shortly after His Resurrection, Christ appeared to His apostles gathered together in their hiding place in Jerusalem. But the apostle Thomas was not with them when Jesus came. When he returned, the other apostles said to him, "*We have seen the Lord.*" *But he said to them, "Unless I see in his hands the print of the nails, and put my finger into the place of the nails, and put my hand into his side, I will not believe.*" The next time that Jesus appeared to His disciples Thomas was with them. *Then He said to Thomas, "Bring here thy finger, and see my hands; and bring here thy hand, and put it into my side; and be not unbelieving, but believing." Thomas answered and said to Him, "My Lord and my God!" Jesus said to him, "Because thou hast seen me, thou hast believed. Blessed are they who have not seen, and yet have believed" (John 20:24–29).*

A Reasonable Faith

For several years, presumably, you have been studying about the doctrinal and moral teachings of the Catholic Church and about her worship, government, and history. Your catechisms and textbooks have presented all this information fully and objectively in an expository way. Possessed of the precious gift of divine faith through baptism, you have rightly accepted these doctrinal and moral teachings as taught by the Church. In the Catholic Church you see the organization founded by Jesus Christ almost two thousand years ago and you recognize this Church as His living spokesman in the world today.

Although you accept unquestionably the full "deposit of faith" as proposed by the Catholic Church, your faith is not blind and unreasoning. It calls into play your understanding and free will. Once you are satisfied that God has revealed the truths proposed to you through the Church, you have the strongest possible grounds for belief because God cannot deceive you or be Himself deceived. Your faith is a reasonable faith and under ordinary circumstances it is entirely adequate for all your personal needs. It will enable you to love and serve God in this world and to work out your salvation for the next world.

But the times are not ordinary. You are living in an environment in which there are many who do not share your Catholic Faith. There are those who question the very bases of your beliefs. Sooner or later you will be brought into contact with those who do not believe in God and doubt that man has an immortal soul and a future destiny of reward or punishment. Not only do they fail to recognize the divine institution of the Catholic Church, but they may even scoff at the Church and ridicule the very idea of religion. Then there are others who are sorely troubled by their doubts and are honest seekers after truth.

Under such circumstances it is both desirable and necessary to delve more deeply into the reasons that underlie certain fundamental truths with which you are already familiar and which you have always accepted on faith. Fortunately some of these truths can be demonstrated by logical reasoning without appealing directly to revelation and faith.

The Apologetic Approach

The science which has for its purpose the explanation and defense of fundamental truths of Christianity is called *apologetics.* It is a *reasoned* explanation of those truths about God and religion which can be known without the aid of supernatural revelation. It goes to the very foundation of things and shows how, with the use of reason, we can arrive at the certainty that the claims of the Catholic Church are true and that she has a right to teach with authority. In doing so, apologetics shows that our faith is trustworthy and provides scientific vindication for believing in the Catholic religion. It enables us to give reasons for the faith that is in us. It answers the question: "Why should I be a Catholic?" The term *apologetics* must not be confused with the common use of the word *apology,* which is employed as an expression of regret for some remark or act, or as an excuse for the absence of something. Webster's Dictionary[1] defines apologetics as a "systematic argumentative discourse in defense, especially of the divine origin and authority of Christianity." In this sense an *apology* implies no admission of guilt or error—quite the contrary!

In the study of apologetics we deal with such fundamental truths as the existence of a Supreme Being who is the Creator of the universe, the existence of a spiritual and immortal soul in man, the need that man has to practice religion and the

[1] Merriam-Webster's *New Collegiate Dictionary*

necessity of a divine revelation to keep him from going astray, the existence of Jesus Christ as both God and man, and, finally, the identification of the Church which Christ founded with the command that all men should hold membership therein. In establishing the validity of all these truths, reliance is placed upon sound reasoning rather than on the authority of faith and revelation.

However, as we take up a study of these truths, basing our investigation for the time being on reason alone and not counting on revelation, let us be perfectly clear about the importance of faith in our own lives. We who have the gift of the Catholic Faith do not take up this study of apologetics because we have any doubts about what our faith teaches. Rather do we study apologetics that we may delve more deeply into the bedrock and reasons for our faith, thus better to understand and treasure our faith so that greater appreciation may stimulate greater love. One who understands the arguments for his faith is less likely to be influenced harmfully by the secular and pagan environment in which he may find himself. He is also better able to protect his faith in contacts with those steeped in doubt and unbelief.

One who has studied apologetics should also be able to carry out more effectively his role as an apostle. Thus he should be in a position to answer the questions and difficulties of honest inquirers or at least he will know where to find the answers. Furthermore, the Catholic layman who has an intelligent knowledge of his religion and who practices it faithfully can have a tremendous influence for good among non-Catholic friends and acquaintances.

The Apologetic Argument

It will be to our advantage to survey briefly the principal points to be proved in the apologetic argument. We begin by proving the existence of God and move on in orderly sequence until we have proved that the Catholic Church is the Church established by Christ and to which He wills all to belong. The complete sequence as developed by apologetics reads as follows:

A Supreme Being is the creator of the universe and all that is in it, including man. He is an all-wise, all-powerful, infinite, and personal God. (Chapters two, three and four.)

As a favored creature of God, man has not only a material body but also a spiritual and immortal soul, with an eternal destiny of everlasting reward, to be won by fulfilling God's purpose in creation. (Chapter five.)

To attain this eternal destiny man must acknowledge his dependence on God by suitable acts of worship. The recognition of this relationship of man with his Creator, we call religion. (Chapter six.)

In order that this religion may effectively assist man to attain his eternal destiny there must be guidance from God, because man left to himself with only natural religion is prone to go astray. This guidance from God we call supernatural revelation *because it makes known to man, on divine authority, the truths of religion. Since it is so necessary for man that God reveal His will, it seems most fitting that He do so. There are many claims to such revelations, so the problem is to distinguish the true from the false. This involves a careful search into the life and teaching of anyone who claims to convey revelation from God.* (Chapter seven.)

The greatest and most perfect teacher of revelation from God is Jesus Christ. We must study His life and seek proof that the revelation He taught is really from God. Our chief sources for the life and teachings of Christ are the documents known as the Four Gospels. Before we can put confidence in what these Gospels tell us of Christ, we must prove them to be reliable historical documents. (Chapter eight.)

Having done this, we find in these Gospels abundant information about the life and teachings of Christ, and also convincing proofs that He was not only a man and the messenger of God, but that He was Himself divine, the true Son of God. (Chapters nine, ten and eleven.)

We find also that He founded a permanent organization which He called His Church, and over which He appointed apostles, with Peter as their head, to rule and govern, to preach the Gospel, and to sanctify all members of the human race. He promised that this church would be an infallible guide to men, that it would be indestructible because He would be with it all days even to the end of time. This church must still exist in the world today as a permanent and infallible guide to men. (Chapter twelve.)

Christ's Church can be identified, by the marks which He bestowed upon it, as the Catholic Church which recognizes the Bishop of Rome, the successor of St. Peter, as its supreme ruler. It is through this Church that Christ wills all men to be saved. Once we recognize this Church as Christ's Church, we have the obligation to seek membership in it, to accept and to live in accordance with its teachings, if we wish to attain our eternal destiny in heaven. (Chapter thirteen.)

The apologetic argument as just outlined can help to prepare the way for one properly disposed to receive from God the gift of the Catholic Faith. There are a series of propositions to be proved consecutively one by one. Each proof prepares the way for the succeeding proposition which must then submit to proof in turn. All of the propositions are joined together like the separate rungs of a ladder. This "apologetic ladder," resting on a foundation of reason, leads from unbelief to belief, from the abyss of atheism to the door of the Church, through which only divine faith can bid one enter. There are eight steps to our ladder, each step a proposition capable of being proved from reason. We will mount one step at a time by proving each proposition completely before going on to the next until we shall have reached our objective, the Catholic Church, at the top of the ladder.

Propositions to be Proved

We have grouped under three headings the eight propositions which we hope to prove. *Catholic* apologetics embraces all eight propositions, including the last two which make it evident that the Catholic Church is the one true Church. Those propositions which should be common to all Christians, Catholic and Protestant, we have listed under *Christian* apologetics. Finally, those propositions which are normally the common belief of Catholics, Protestants and Jews, we have listed under *Natural* apologetics.

These are the propositions to be proved in succeeding chapters:

Catholic Apologetics (1–8)
Christian Apologetics (1–6)
Natural Apologetics (1–4)

1. That there is a Supreme Being, the Creator of the universe, who is an infinite, eternal, all-wise, all-good, all-powerful, and personal God. (Chapters two, three and four.)
2. That every man has a spiritual and immortal soul which has an eternal destiny. (Chapter five.)
3. That every man must acknowledge his dependence on God by suitable acts of religion (worship). (Chapter six.)
4. That an acceptable natural religion is not possible for man and, therefore, a supernatural religion is necessary which God can and has revealed to man. (Chapter seven.)
5. That the Four Gospels are reliable historical documents which give information about Jesus Christ, the chief claimant to, and the chief teacher of revelation. (Chapter eight.)
6. That a final and complete revelation was made through Jesus Christ, who was both God and man. (Chapters nine, ten and eleven.)
7. That Jesus Christ founded a Church with Peter as the first head, and that this Church still exists because it was to be infallible and indestructible and has certain other convincing marks or characteristics by which it may be identified. (Chapter twelve.)
8. That the Catholic Church is *the* Church which Christ founded to offer to men the means of salvation and to which He wills all men to belong. (Chapter thirteen.)

Apologetics, a Mental Discipline

To get something out of the study of apologetics you must apply yourself diligently. But in doing so you must avoid the temptation merely to memorize. Instead, reason things out carefully until you have completely grasped the idea and the nature of the proof that is required. Then strive to arrange your thoughts in logical sequence before you commit yourself to speech or writing.

For many students apologetics is not an easy subject to grasp. It seems interesting enough to read or to discuss in class. But when you try, in a recitation or quiz, to put to use what you think you have learned, it is not so simple as it appears. Apologetics requires careful, connected, and accurate thinking. Furthermore, it requires the ability to express one's self exactly. Here many fall down.

The study of geometry has much in common with the study of apologetics. Both demand logical reasoning ability. Geometry applies logical reasoning to tangible or visible things, like lines, planes or solids. Apologetics applies logical reasoning to intangibles, for the most part, like God and His attributes, man's soul, and spiritual faculties. Apologetics accustoms one to logical thinking and will train one in argumentation. It will give one the ability to state his case clearly and then to back it up with convincing proofs.

Apologetics, an Aid to the Lay Apostolate

Today the apostolate of bringing men to accept the true Church of Christ must operate on different levels. In the United States in recent years, Catholics, Protestants and Jews have been coming together on a high level of intellectual and religious leadership to argue and discuss those things which are their common concern and to endeavor to reach rational conclusions. In Europe, notably Germany, Catholic and Protestant theologians have met from time to time to discuss calmly their doctrinal differences.

Discussions of this type have been called *dialogs*, probably to remove them from the realm of debate, a form of argumentation in which one seeks by his arguments to overcome his opponent and register a victory. In *dialog* the effort is made to explain one's point of view clearly and to understand that which gives rise to differing points of view. To be successful it must be conducted with patience and be founded on charity, knowledge and understanding, and good will.

Similar patience, charity, knowledge and understanding, and good will must mark the day-to-day contacts which afford opportunity for the lay apostolate, the attempt to bring Christ into the market place and into the lives of friends and acquaintances. You may, for instance, have an opportunity to bring Christ and the Church to the attention of one who does not believe in the existence of God but welcomes the opportunity to hear presented the case for belief in God.

If you wish to succeed in presenting your argument, you must try to understand the situation of your hearer and then make your explanations and proofs clear and convincing to him. Do not make wild or general statements and then jump to your conclusion. Develop your argument patiently and logically, using comparisons and examples freely to drive home your points.

You cannot take anything for granted in this kind of argumentation. You cannot assume that your hearer will readily accept truths which you see clearly. Hence you must begin with ideas that he can readily understand and then lead him on patiently, step by step, to the truth which you are endeavoring to prove. For example: You believe in the existence of God. You have always believed in God. You have the gift of faith, and the existence of God is as certain to you as anything can be. However, if you are trying to convince one who does not believe in God that God, in fact, exists, you have to start with truths held by your hearer and then lead up logically to your proof for the existence of a Supreme Being. This we hope you will be able to do, at least with moderate success, by the time you have completed your course in apologetics.

A Word of Caution

We have considered the relative importance of divine faith and of the human reason employed in apologetics, and have outlined the truths which are to be proved. Before taking up these proofs one by one, there is a word of caution to be spoken, especially to the man of strong faith.

When we accept truths on the word of God, who can neither deceive us nor be Himself deceived, we have the strongest possible motive for belief. When these same truths are presented to us for belief on the testimony of reason alone, the chances are that we may not be overly impressed if we already have a strong and lively faith. Nevertheless, to one who has weak faith or who has no faith, the reasoning of apologetics may be very convincing and may serve to strengthen faith or to prepare the way for faith.

An analogy from human faith may help to clarify this thought. If one has a valued and trusted friend in whose qualities of mind and heart one has implicit confidence, the reasoned and logical testimony of a third party to the qualities and virtues of this friend will seem to fall far short of the reality, no matter how convincing the testimony may be to a stranger. Such testimony on behalf of one's friend would, no doubt, be welcomed for the good it might do for others.

In somewhat similar fashion the man of faith may be unimpressed personally by the reasoning of apologetics because his knowledge through faith is stronger. However, there are other compensations in apologetics for the man of faith. It is a joy to learn how these fundamental truths of faith can be so convincingly demonstrated by reason. It gives a boost to the morale, so to speak, and serves to strengthen faith. It gives the man of faith more confidence and should stimulate his zeal in dealing with the skeptic and the unbeliever. It provides a common platform on which to discuss matters with them. Besides, it is consoling to see how clearly it can be proved to the "outsider," from reason alone, that the Catholic Church is without question the Church which Christ established to bring salvation to all mankind.

REVIEW QUESTIONS

1. What is *faith,* in general, and why is it so important?
2. What is *human faith?*
3. What is *divine faith?*
4. Why are both *human faith* and *divine faith* necessary?
5. What is meant by "reasonable" faith?
6. Why is belief founded on divine faith stronger than belief on human faith?
7. How do we know that it is more "blessed" to believe on divine faith than to believe only on the evidence of positive proof?
8. What do you understand by the ability to "give reason for the faith that is in you"?
9. Write a short version of the prayer, "An Act of Faith."
10. Give a definition for apologetics.
11. Name two religious truths that come within the scope of apologetics and two that do not come within its scope.
12. Why does apologetics make no use of revelation and divine faith?
13. How does apologetics differ from previous religion courses?
14. Give two solid reasons for studying apologetics.
15. Of what practical use is the study of apologetics?
16. How can apologetics help you in your contacts with non-Catholics?
17. What are the fundamental truths with which apologetics deals?
18. Where does apologetics begin and where does it end?
19. What analogy has been used to illustrate the method and function of apologetics?
20. What proof is the high point in the apologetic argument?
21. What proof is the ultimate objective of apologetics?

SUGGESTIONS FOR READING

"The Catholic and the Liberal Society," *America,* John Cogley, July 4, 1959, Vol. CI, No. 14, Whole Number 2614, pp. 492–496.

Why it Pays to be a Catholic, D. J. Corrigan, C.SS.R. Liguorian Pamphlets, Liguori, Missouri, 1957. 31 pp., 10¢. (One is a Catholic because he is convinced of the truth of the Catholic religion. However, for a Catholic there are many compensations that help to keep him faithful to his duties. This booklet lists and discusses sixteen such compensations.)

Why I am a Catholic, James F. Cunningham, C.S.P. The Paulist Press, 401 West 59th Street, New York 19, N.Y., 1938. 40 pp., 10¢.

These Unreasonable Catholics, Glenn Herzog, O.F.M. Cap. Catholic Information Society, 214 West 31st Street, New York 1, N.Y. 15 pp., 5¢. (In believing on faith one does not abandon the use of reason.)

I Believe, Wilfred G. Hurley, C.S.P. The Paulist Press, 1935. 212 pp., 75¢, pp. 1–101. (Beginning with proof for the existence of God, this book arrives, step by step, at the conviction that Christ's Church is the Catholic Church. Then it explains the principal teachings of that Church.)

Certainly I'm A Catholic! Thomas A. McDermott. Milwaukee: The Bruce Publishing Company, 1950. 154 pp. (A young Catholic lawyer, noting some of the "material" disadvantages of being a Catholic and that some Catholics have apparently succumbed to this lure, proceeds to reason out: "Why am I a Catholic?" Recognizing that such replies as "you were born a Catholic," "you were educated in Catholic schools," or "you received the gift of Catholic Faith," are only partial answers, he considers the attitude of the Catholic Church on the basic questions and problems of the day and concludes that he is, and will continue to be a Catholic because the Catholic system of thought and way of life provide the only reasonable and consistent answers to the basic questions and problems troubling him and all mankind.)

Why I am a Catholic, D. F. Miller, C.SS.R. Liguorian Pamphlets, 1958. 23 pp., 10¢. (In giving reasons "Why I am a Catholic" it also tells how and why one should become a Catholic.)

Faith is Your Only Answer, Richard Walsh, C.S.P. The Paulist Press. 28 pp., 10¢.

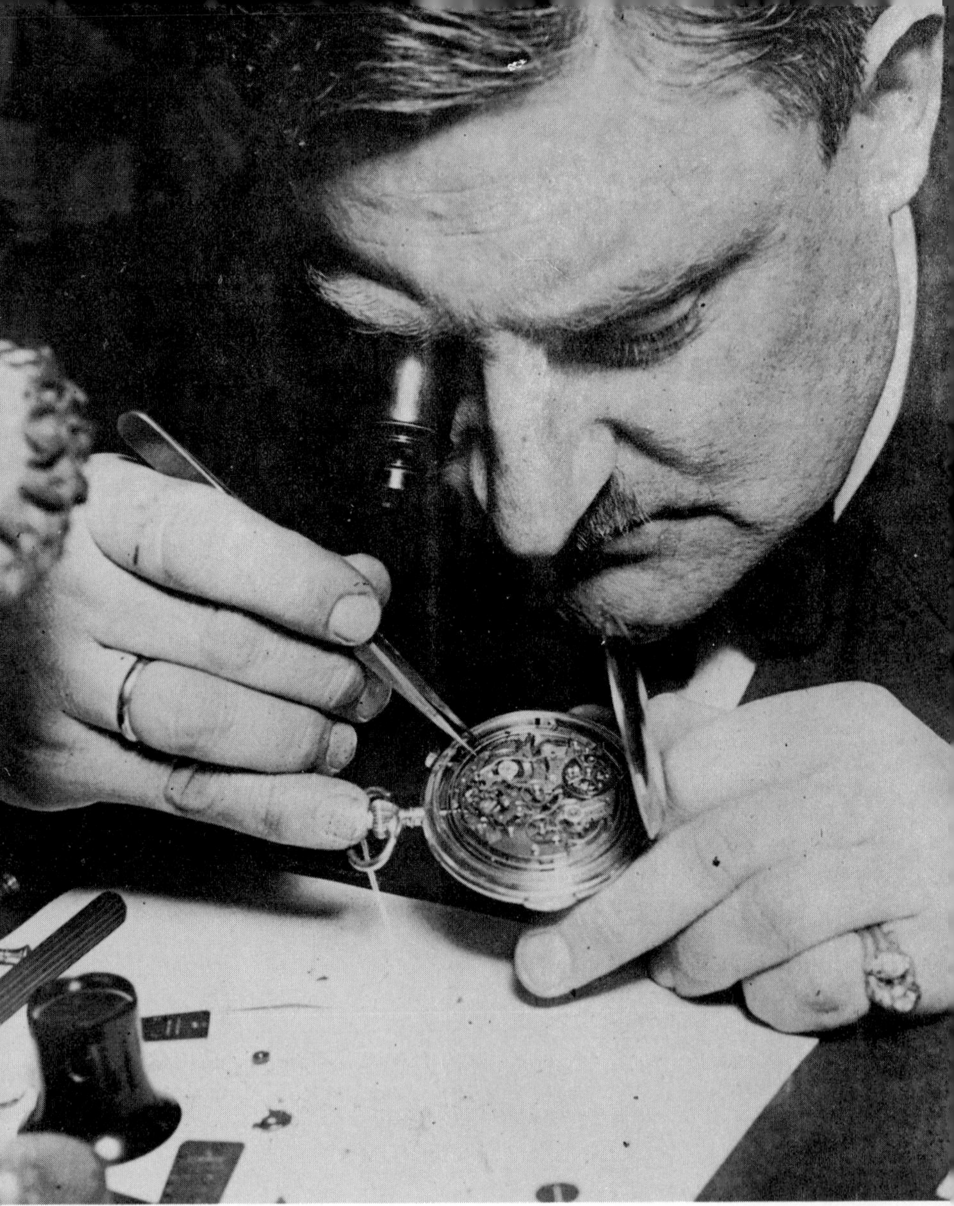

FPG photo

A watchmaker at work. Even though we never saw a watchmaker at work we would know from examining the watch that he did exist and that he had the ability to put the intricate parts of the watch together with great precision and skill.

The universe, a much more complicated mechanism, operates with such precision that we set our clocks by it. The unseen designer of the universe is God, whose existence is just as certainly known from His creation as is the watchmaker's from his watch.

Chapter 2

God exists, I

The Reasonableness of Belief in God

THE FIRST TASK IN apologetics is to prove that there is a Supreme Being, a God who is the Creator of the universe and all that is contained therein. The existence of God is, of course, the foundation upon which the science of apologetics rests. It is obvious, therefore, that the evidence for God's existence should be abundant and so clear and plain that even the most ignorant savage could get the idea.

Everyone believes in the existence of a Supreme Being, that is, practically everyone, except those peculiar individuals who do not, or say they do not, believe in God. It may be that they cannot reason rightly, or they have managed to close their eyes so tightly as to shut out completely all light of evidence. Of course there will be some who through false education or environment are temporarily without belief in God. But if they are earnest and sincere and have an open mind, they will undoubtedly see the light in God's own good time. These are the ones for whom we should have the most kindly solicitude, because we may be able to help them through our ability to demonstrate clearly the existence of God.

This abundant evidence for the existence of God can be marshalled under several chief headings or arguments, any one of which is calculated to lead to the conviction that there is a God, provided that one is prepared to follow the reasoning with an open mind. All arguments will not be equal in their appeal. Thus, if one has a flair for the sciences, the proofs which draw more heavily on scientific knowledge, such as the arguments from design, physical law, and motion, will be more interesting and convincing. If one leans more toward the liberal or humanistic studies, the arguments from conscience, contingency, causality, and the universal belief of mankind may be more attractive. Separately, each one of the arguments presents a good case for the existence of God. Cumulatively, they should be overwhelmingly convincing. We shall consider here three arguments, namely, the argument drawn from the evidence of order and design apparent in the world, the argument based on the existence of physical laws binding all created things, and finally, the argument drawn from moral law (conscience) binding only man. For those who can readily master these arguments and wish further food for thought, additional arguments for the existence of God will be found in the following chapter.

The Evidence of Order and Design

In the works of nature as well as in the works of man there are abundant evidences of order or orderly arrangement and of design. Before going any further, let us define our terms. By *order* we mean that things have been purposely arranged, organized or put in their proper places, especially in relation to each other or to other things. By *design* we mean that something has been fashioned according to a plan and for a purpose. The two words are closely allied and are used interchangeably in our discussion. Thus *design* may be said to be the planning of order just as *order* may be called the result of design.

Now order (or design) does not just happen. It is not the result of accident or chance. It requires intelligence. When, for instance, four rods of equal length are found laid out on the floor to form a perfect square, we know that some intelligent being put them there. They did not happen to fall that way by chance or accident. In fact, it is hardly possible that they came to be four rods of equal length by chance or accident. Some intelligent being cut them to size or selected them of a size in the first place. If this be so with four simple rods arranged to form a simple square, it is all the more true of complicated arrangements.

Thus we are justified in stating as a general conclusion the following principle: *Distinctive order or design presupposes the existence of an intelligent designer.* A little reflection will show that this is really a self-evident truth. It is this reasonable assumption which underlies our proof for the existence of God, drawn from the evidence of order and design in the universe.

The Proof from Order or Design

We are now ready to formulate the proof for the existence of God, drawn from the evidence of order and design in the universe.

In all man-made things about us, we readily see undeniable evidence of intelligent human designers who planned them, and of intelligent human artisans who fashioned them. The more complicated and ingenious are the objects we behold, the more we pay tribute to the intelligence and skill of the men who designed and fashioned these objects. The fact that we may never know or see these human designers and artisans does not in any way diminish our belief in their existence.

Take a wrist watch, for instance. It is an attractive little mechanism. It is made up of a number of small parts of various shapes and sizes, each carefully machined and polished, and put together skillfully so that the whole, working in unison, measures efficiently the passage of time. The watch clearly was fashioned for this very purpose. Since order and design are apparent in this watch, we know with certainty that it did not just happen to be. *Somebody made it.* Since the watch was made to tell time, somebody *knew what he was doing* when he made it. Somebody *had a purpose* in making it. No one could convince you that this is all the result of chance, that the parts of the watch happened to fall together this way, and then the mechanism began to tell time. You would rightly consider such an explanation to be impossible and ridiculous. The only explanation that makes sense is that someone with intelligence, who had a purpose, made the watch. The fact that you did not see the watch made or that you have no idea who made it, does not lessen your conviction that it was made by an intelligent being.

We could repeat this reasoning with a thousand and one objects which have been fashioned by the mind and hand of man (Example 1). In every instance the order and design we observe point irresistibly to an intelligent designer, known or unknown.

When we come to consider the thousand and one objects around us that are far beyond the intelligence and powers of man to fashion, such as the flowers and trees, the birds of the air, the beasts of the field, even man himself, with all his wonderful faculties (Example 2), our line of reasoning need not change. Wherever there is order and design there must be an intelligent designer back of it all. But now the designer must have superhuman intelligence and unlimited powers. He is the Supreme Designer, the Supreme Architect, the Almighty God.

When we look from earth into the heavens and behold all the marvels of sun and moon and stars which no man made or ever can make, and see how these wonders dwarf man-made objects, we stand in awe of the infinite intelligence and power of the Great Designer, the Supreme Creator, God, who made all these things. If we do not see God, the Creator of the universe, in visible form, we apprehend Him no less truly in His works which are all about us.

If it is unthinkable to try to explain the man-made wrist watch by saying that it made itself or came together by chance, it is all the more absurd to try to explain the universe and all the wonders of nature without an all-wise omnipotent Creator.

Examples of Order and Design

Example 1. *Order and Design, Human and Divine.* Suppose we pay a visit to a cabinet maker's shop on a Sunday. There is no one at work or in sight, but the shop is clean and everything is in order. Racks are stocked with clean, fresh wood of various lengths and sizes. There are also tools and machines that are shiny and bright and free from rust. The order and neatness of the place create in us a very favorable impression of the cabinet maker whose shop this is and to whom we unhesitatingly attribute all this order. We would think it fantastically absurd (and rightly so!) if it were suggested to us that all this order was the result of a chance happening, a mere accident. Such an explanation is preposterous! Why try to take the credit away from one to whom it is so clearly and justly due?

Suppose a few days later we return again to this shop after working hours, when no one is about. We observe that the lumber stock has been noticeably depleted. But now there are several very attractive end tables to be seen. Two are apparently complete, with the beautiful grain of the oak wood showing to good advantage beneath the highly polished surface. The remaining tables are in varying stages of completion. Could we possibly imagine that the beautiful cabinet work which we see here is only the product of mere chance? Do we not recognize it at once for what it is: the handiwork of a skilled and intelligent artisan? Can we not almost see the hand of the artisan moving lovingly over the finished surface to detect any roughness or irregularity?

But stop a minute! What about the human hand that played such an important part in accomplishing the cabinet maker's design for the end table? Actually that human hand is a far more wonderful example of order and ingenuity than any or all of the tables or tools or machines in that shop. That hand which moves with such freedom and ease and precision is quite complicated and remarkable even though it is only one organ of the human body. It is fashioned of flesh and blood, of bones, muscles, tendons, and nerves. We are told that the framework of the hand is composed of no less than nineteen bones of various sizes and shapes, all delicately formed, while eight more bones of various shapes provide strength and flexibility in the wrist. Even the slightest movement of the hand causes a highly complicated and intricate interplay of bones and muscles and tendons so that they contract here or relax there, strain or slacken to suit the need of the moment. Nevertheless the several units work together harmoniously for the production of each and every wave or grip or movement of the hand. Moreover the hand as part of the body whole can repair its own cuts, abrasions and bruises, even mend its broken bones. Surely *blind chance* is no explanation for these marvels.

Whence then, has this come about? It could not happen by chance. Nor could man perfect the hand either for himself or for anyone else, because it grows and develops uniquely with each individual. But there must be an author of this wonderful piece of mechanism who has caused it to grow to its present shape, to develop so many tissues, and to attain such efficiency. There is only one answer! The human hand was made by the great Master-Worker, Almighty God, who has made this and the countless other marvels with which this world is filled.

Example 2. *The Wonders of the Camera, the Human Eye and the Living Cell.* The man-made camera and the human eye have something in common. They are both designed to record an image of what we can see. The camera does this by admitting light through a lens in a circular opening of the camera box in such a way that a picture of that which we wish to represent is imprinted on a sensitive plate. The human eye has a parallel mechanism and similar function. But how much more marvelous by comparison! Thus the eyeball corresponds to the camera box, the crystalline lens of the eye to the camera lens, and the retina to the sensitized film. In both instances several distinct things are found joined or fitted together to produce a single result, namely, a clear picture on the sensitized film and on the retina.

Now the camera was made by a man who assembled the materials required and then shaped, fitted and polished them with great skill. Though we greatly admire his skill, it is quite probable that we could duplicate the work with proper training and practice. But never, under any circumstances, could we hope to make a human eye. This is the handiwork of a superhuman Being who, in some mysterious way which we are quite unable to understand, caused a minute particle of flesh to multiply itself a million times over, and, in so doing, gradually to build up, shape, and perfect every part of this wonderful human eye. We are quick to recognize that this is far beyond the possibility of human imitation.

But the eye is only one of the marvelous organs of the human body. The entire body with its flesh and blood, its bone and muscle, and its various limbs and organs, is formed in precisely the same way. Thus, man's body begins as a single living cell which multiplies itself and gradually forms all the complex organs and interrelated systems of nerves and veins and arteries.

Small as it is, that living cell is far more wonderful than any machine that man ever made. We can see, for example, how a watch does its work. We can trace the movement of the spring as it passes from one part to another, until finally it is communicated to the hands of the watch. But we are unable to fathom how the living cell does its work. All that we can do is to bow in humble reverence and admiration before the intelligence and power of God who can give to a living cell the ability to produce the wonderful faculties of man: his sight, his hearing and his other senses—the complete man, capable himself of making wonderful machines.

The Proof from Physical Law

Law, in general, has been defined as an ordinance of reason made by the proper authority for the common good. This definition refers specifically to man-made laws of which we have many kinds. Laws are necessary for good order in any community. Without laws we would have confusion and chaos. Thus traffic will not move smoothly or safely through the streets of a city unless there are traffic laws promulgated by competent authority and obeyed by the general public. Even the modern superhighway, which is the last word in convenience and improved safety design, will have its utility and safety largely nullified if there are no traffic regulations. We are accustomed to these man-made laws and we correctly attribute them to the human lawgivers who made these laws to preserve order in human society. Never for an instant would we consider that these laws established themselves or that they were the product of chance. We recognize that a law must have a lawgiver.

But all nature is guided by laws which we call *physical* to distinguish them from another type of law which we call *moral*. Everywhere we see evidence of a multitude of these laws governing nature in all its physical aspects, both living and nonliving. Everywhere there is order. Everywhere there is admirable arrangement. Everywhere there are fixed modes of action because of these laws. The physical sciences, like physics, chemistry, and astronomy, show that nonliving matter, from the stars of heaven to the smallest speck of dust, are subject to fixed laws in all their movements and changes. The same holds for living things, plants, animals, and men. Each species grows, develops, and acts in the way that is peculiar to its own kind.

Many times there is conflict between man-made laws, and sometimes they are honored more in the breach than in observance. But the laws of nature are unfailing in their regularity and observance. Furthermore they are established in accord with a marvelous master plan that provides for perfect harmony among these laws. The entire universe is bound together into one vastly complicated whole, and is like a great machine, the parts of which are admirably fitted together (Example 3). The orderly movement of the heavens, the marvelous structure of living things and their organs, the wonderful instinct (Example 4) of the lower animals, as instanced in the work of insects and the nest building of birds—all these marvels are the products of nature's laws. The wisdom, foresight, and harmony of these physical laws (Example 5) infinitely surpass any man-made laws. Since it would be unthinkable to suppose that the universe made its own laws or to attempt to ascribe these laws to the operation of chance, we must see back of all these laws a Supreme Lawgiver of infinite intelligence and power, whom we call God.

Examples of Physical Law

Example 3. *Physical Laws Are Everywhere.* "We find ourselves on the surface of a tiny satellite, whirling upon its axis at the rate of a thousand miles an hour. Although we feel no motion, not only are we turning thus, but are also being borne along our planet's path around the sun with a velocity of 1,080 miles a minute, or *one and a half million miles a day!* . . .

"And what we do in our small corner of the universe, millions of other suns and satellites are doing—swinging in perfect equilibrium millions of miles from one another, and moving with such perfect regularity that most of their vast changes can be foretold to a minute centuries in advance, or ascertained at any date of the historic past!

"Yet the same law that guides the motion of Arcturus regulates the falling leaf. The same Divine hand paints the sunset glory and the petals of the rose. Proofs of design and wisdom, which overpower one in his study of astronomy, are just as evident in every other sphere of science. The revelations of the microscope are as marvelous as those of the telescope. The same supreme Intelligence is discoverable in the infinitely small as in the infinitely great. The ornithologist finds an adaptation of means to ends in the wonderful structure of birds; the zoologist traces it in every form of animal life; the botanist is filled with reverence and admiration in his investigation of the fertilization of flowers; the worker in the laboratory is lost in wonder at the mysteries of chemical affinities" (Stoddard, *Rebuilding a Lost Faith,* pp. 35–36).

Example 4. *The Marvelous Instinct of Animals.* "The lower animals in the work they do, often exhibit instances of wonderful order. They perform with great skill a series of actions for the achievement of a definite purpose. Take the following example: There is a kind of sand-wasp (the ammophila hirsuta) which prepares a worm as food for its larvae by cutting as with a surgical lance and paralyzing all the motor-nerve centers, so as to deprive the worm of movement but not of life. The sand-wasp then lays its eggs beside the worm and covers all with clay. It has got its surgical skill without instruction or practice. It lives for but one season. It has not been taught by its parents, for it has never seen them. It does not teach its offspring, because it dies before they emerge from the earth" (Sheehan, *Apologetics and Catholic Doctrine,* p. 15).

This marvelous ability which the sand-wasp exhibits, and the similar abilities which all nonrational creatures possess in greater or lesser degree, were implanted in them as instincts by God. It was He who planned the work. It is He who moves the insect to perform it.

Example 5. *Animate Matter Is Subject to, and Served by, the Laws of Inanimate Matter.* "All living things are subject to the laws of inanimate matter. Nutrition, growth, and many other processes take place in accordance with the laws of chemistry. The laws of gravitation and energy are as valid for the living as for the nonliving. The tree, for instance, which stores up the energy of the sun's rays, returns it later on when its withered branches burn on the hearth.

"Animate matter is served by the laws of inanimate matter. Examples: Gravitation has so placed the earth in relation to the sun that it receives the moderate quantity of light and heat necessary for the support of organic life. . . . The air contains in every 100 parts nearly 79 of nitrogen and 21 of oxygen gas, together with .04 of carbonic acid, a minute proportion of ammonia and other constituents, and a variable quantity of watery vapour. In pure nitrogen, man would suffocate; in pure oxygen, his body would burn out rapidly like a piece of tinder; without carbonic acid plant life would be impossible. . . . The plant exhales oxygen and inhales carbonic acid; the animal exhales carbonic acid, and inhales oxygen: thus, each ministers to the life of the other. . . . Bodies contract with a fall of temperature, and yet water expands when its temperature falls below 4° Centigrade. Hence, ice is lighter than water, and forms a surface-covering which, being of low conductivity, prevents the rapid congealing of the entire body of water and the destruction of living things beneath" (Sheehan, *Apologetics and Catholic Doctrine,* pp. 13–14).

The Proof from Conscience

Man's body is subject to the physical laws of the universe in the same way as any other physical body. But man is more than a physical body. He has spiritual powers of intellect and free will which distinguish him from all the animal creation. Through his intellect, man has a power which gives him knowledge of both what is good and what is evil. Through his will he has the power to do or not to do that which his intellect proposes to him. This power of choosing which man possesses is capable of great good or great harm. If man were to be left entirely to himself, without any guidance whatever, and failed to use wisely this fateful gift of free choice, this deficiency might bring more confusion to the world than would even the absence of all physical laws.

The Moral Law. But there is a law guiding man in his choice of what to do. Impressed on his heart are certain dictates of reason which make known that certain things are right and other things are wrong. This law is called the *moral* law. This moral law is made known to us by our intellect, which sees the rightness or wrongness of the thing we wish to do. It governs the intellect and will of man by telling him that he must do the things that are good, such as being just, truthful, and considerate of others; and that he must avoid the things that are evil, such as being untruthful, unjust, and inconsiderate of others.

Conscience. This act of the intellect, by which we judge what is morally good or bad, is called conscience. Although conscience is correctly defined as the act of the intellect by which we judge what is morally good or morally evil, we think of it more familiarly as the little voice inside us that says we *must* do or avoid certain things. This voice of conscience cannot be wheedled or cajoled. It cannot be bribed or coerced, ignored or entirely silenced. It *can* be disobeyed, for man is a free agent, but it cannot be disobeyed with impunity. Conscience does not advise, it commands. It threatens us with punishment if we disobey. If we have transgressed, it will give us no peace. It pricks us with self-reproach and gnaws us with remorse (Example 6). If we obey, on the contrary, it rewards us with the peace and happiness which is sometimes called "the testimony of a good conscience."

One can, it is true, acquire a distorted or warped conscience because of various circumstances with which we have no need to deal here. In such an instance the conscience, subjectively, will function in the same way although, objectively, it may not be a reliable guide. Also, by constantly doing violence to conscience, one may drown out the still, small voice for a while. But it is a voice that is seldom silent for very long and can never be entirely hushed.

This prompting of conscience, either approving or disapproving, is one of the most universal of human experiences. It is common to all men everywhere. Both pagan and Christian philosophers bear testimony to it in almost identical terms.

Whence comes this conscience possessed of such peculiar characteristics? It cannot arise as a consequence of laws which man makes for himself, or because society has said that certain things are morally right or wrong. For conscience is frequently at odds with a man's own wishes and also at variance with the dictates of society. It acts independently of the praise or blame of others. Moreover, it points unerringly to One who watches over us and knows even our most secret thoughts and desires. The fact that there is no human witness whatever to one's good or evil deed is no deterrent to conscience. Conscience knows that there is One who sees and who will approve or disapprove.

There is only one possible explanation for the phenomenon of conscience with its automatic response, its peculiar characteristics, and its universality. It can owe its existence only to an invisible lawgiver of great intelligence and power in whose eyes there is a difference between good and evil, who gave man an intellect capable of seeing this difference, and who makes his will known to man through conscience. This lawgiver must be most wise and good, for wisdom and goodness appear everywhere in this moral law. He must be also most powerful, for he can make known his wishes to all men through conscience without the use of any words. This supreme, all-wise, and all-powerful lawgiver can be none other than God.

As one might expect, there have been Christian writers who consider the fact of conscience and the moral law to be one of the strongest reasons in proof of the existence of God. It is interesting to note that many pre-Christian writers have also looked upon the phenomenon of conscience as one of the clearest evidences of God's existence. "From the consciousness of moral obligation which we find implanted in us," wrote Aristotle, "we reason back to its eternal Source—the Infinite and Perfect." Seneca wrote: "Every man has a judge and witness of all the good and evil that he does. . . . God is nigh to thee, he is with thee, he is within thee. . . . an observer and guardian both of what is good and what is evil in us." Cicero, Epictetus, and Socrates wrote in a similar vein. (Stoddard, *Rebuilding a Lost Faith*, pp. 46–47.)

Examples of the Operation of Conscience

Example 6. *For Conscience' Sake.* Occasionally testimony to the long-range, continuous, prodding effect of conscience will appear in a current news item. There is, for example, the man who killed another under circumstances that completely escaped detection. Although he moved to a distant city, was outwardly successful, and was not even remotely liable to suspicion, the little voice of conscience would not be stilled. Finally, to silence the accusing monitor and to attain the much-desired peace of mind, the killer confessed his crime to the police.

Another instance is the embezzler who has dishonestly acquired some valuable property. Held to be an honored and respected citizen, he has successfully outwitted the law. Although reformed and eminently successful, he cannot find freedom from the silent but persistent accusations of conscience. In the hope of attaining the desired peace of conscience he confesses his wrong. surrenders to the law and declares his wish to make amends.

The Conscience Fund. Municipal, state and federal governments, and probably every large business, are familiar with constantly recurring instances of restitution by anonymous persons urged on by the voice of conscience. Webster's *Unabridged International Dictionary* defines *conscience money* as "money paid to relieve the conscience by rendering or restoring, usually anonymously, what has been wrongfully acquired or held, as a tax payment. Such money paid into the United States Treasury is deposited in what is called the *conscience fund.*"

Additional proofs for the existence of God will be found in chapter three. These proofs may be considered as an extension of this chapter, or they may be considered later if time permits, or they may be omitted altogether at the discretion of the teacher.

REVIEW QUESTIONS

1. Why might one expect to find abundant evidence for the existence of God?
2. What do you mean by *order* in the sense in which the word is used in apologetics? Illustrate with an example.
3. What do you mean by *design?* Illustrate with an example.
4. What is meant by saying that something happens by chance? Illustrate by example.
5. What conclusion is inevitable when one is confronted with evidence of complex order or design?
6. What would the visible presence of the watchmaker contribute to your conviction that your watch is the result of intelligent design?

7. How does evidence of design in the universe prove the existence of God?
8. What work of nature impresses you most with a conviction of God's existence, and why?
9. What do you mean by physical laws? Illustrate with an example.
10. How does the presence of physical laws in the universe prove the existence of God?
11. What is meant by the expression: "there is marvelous harmony in the laws of nature"? Give an example.
12. What do you mean by moral laws? Illustrate with an example.
13. What do you mean by conscience? Give both a popular and a formal definition.
14. How does conscience prove the existence of God?
15. What is meant by saying that the absence of moral laws might bring more confusion to the world than would even the absence of physical laws?
16. How would you counter the assertion that conscience is merely the outgrowth of the customs of society?

SUGGESTIONS FOR READING

"An Ovum Speaks for the Record," *Truths Men Live By,* John A. O'Brien. New York: The Macmillan Company, 1946, Chapter VI, pp. 49–53. (Note (c) below.)

"A Bee Takes the Witness Stand," *Ibid.*, Chapter V, pp. 45–49. (Note (b) below.)

"A Feather Speaks," *Ibid.*, Chapter IV, pp. 33–45.

"The Atom Bears Witness," *Ibid.*, Chapter II, pp. 18–26.

"The Heavens Show Forth," *Ibid.*, Chapter I, pp. 3–18.

"The Human Body Affirms," *Ibid.*, Chapter VII, pp. 53–60.

"The Origin of Life Demands," *Ibid.*, Chapter VIII, pp. 60–62.

"The Testimony of Life," *Ibid.*, Chapter III, pp. 26–33. (Note (a) below.)

"The Voice of Conscience," *Ibid.*, Chapter IX, pp. 62–75.

"Searching for Light," *Rebuilding a Lost Faith,* John L. Stoddard. New York: P. J. Kenedy & Sons, 1924, Chapter IV, pp. 34–43.

The Case for God, Richard Ginder. Catholic Information Society, 214 West 31st Street, New York 1, N.Y. 16 pp., 5¢. (Proofs for God's existence from design, causality, and as the "Prime Mover.")

There is a God, Wilfred G. Hurley, C.S.P. The Paulist Press, 401 West

59th Street, New York 19, N.Y., 1934. 20 pp., 10¢. (Proofs for God's existence from causality, law and order, and conscience.)

(a) *A Leaf Outsmarts Scientists,* John A. O'Brien. Catholic Information Society. 15 pp., 5¢. (Similar to "The Testimony of Life" above. A proof from design and physical law.)

(b) *A Bee Outwits Scientists,* John A. O'Brien. Catholic Information Society. 14 pp., 5¢. (Similar to "A Bee Takes the Witness Stand" above. Another proof from design and physical law.)

(c) *A Baby Bears Witness to God,* John A. O'Brien. The Catholic Information Society. 15 pp., 5¢. (Similar to "An Ovum Speaks for the Record" above. Another proof from design and physical law.)

Bill Jones Meets God, William J. Quinlan. The Catholic Information Society. 14 pp., 5¢. (One who faces death and has time to think will return to God.)

Space and Spirit, Sir Edmund Whittaker. Hinsdale, Illinois: Henry Regnery Co., 1948. 143 pp. (A scientist, a convert to Catholicism, gives arguments for the existence of God in terms of physics and mathematics.)

The Great Design, Frances Mason, editor. New York: Macmillan, 1934. 324 pp. (Several scientists, mostly non-Catholic Europeans, testify to nature's witness to an Intelligent Guiding Hand in the direction of the universe. The material is chiefly from the field of biology and transcends any possible explanation based on purely mechanical forces.)

Science and the Existence of God, Pope Pius XII. America Press, 70 E. 45th Street, New York 17, N.Y., 1959.

Villanova University photo

Chemistry students at work. The physical laws which the Creator established for the universe are the basis for the science of chemistry, as well as for all the natural sciences.

Chapter 3

God exists, II

IN THE PRECEDING chapter we developed rational proofs for the existence of God drawn from the evidence all about us of order and design, of physical law, and of moral law. These proofs were selected because they are easier to grasp and they are readily convincing. We present here four additional proofs which are drawn respectively from the principle of causality, the law of motion, the fact of universal dependence, and the testimony of history. Of these four proofs, the proof from causality and that from motion have to be more closely reasoned and are more difficult to grasp.

All of these proofs for the existence of God, taken singly, are capable of convincing a fair-minded person that God exists. Cumulatively, of course, they have even stronger force. But in neither instance can they be expected to bring the warm, firm, and strong belief in God which divine faith gives.

The Proof from Causality

Everything that we touch or see had a beginning. It did not always exist and it will not continue indefinitely to exist. Whenever a thing does not exist at one time and is later found to exist, there must have been an efficient cause of its existence. By the efficient cause we mean the person or thing that actually makes the thing exist.

The desk we write upon did not always exist. Even though it now does exist, it will not always have a claim on existence. The desk is the result of human labor and skill which cut, cured, and fashioned the wood of the tree into its present useful form. The desk was made by a skilled craftsman. He was the *efficient* cause since he actually produced it from the wood, and the desk is the *effect* of his labor.

Actually everything we touch or see is an *effect* because it was caused by someone or something other than itself. From this we can reason that every effect has a cause. Furthermore, *everything which begins to exist (an effect) must have a reason for its existence outside of itself.* This self-evident truth is known as *the principle of causality.* For if a thing begins to exist, it did not exist at all before this beginning. Something had to bring about its existence and this something could not have been the thing that had not yet begun to exist. With this principle of causality and the apparent absurdity of an endless and infinite progression from effect to cause, we can construct a proof for the existence of God.

The proof from causality for the existence of God can be formulated in outline as follows:

Since everything with which we come in contact had a

beginning, it did not always exist. In reality, therefore, it is an effect which was caused by something apart from itself. Whatever begins to exist must have a reason for its existence outside of itself. This reason must be an efficient cause because it must actually make the effect exist. Now since every effect has a cause, and every cause is in itself the effect of another cause, we come up against a dilemma when we start to trace back from effect to cause. Either we must go back and back and back without end from effect to cause—an infinite progression that is unthinkable—or else we must admit the existence of a *first cause* which was itself uncaused.

This first cause must always have existed, or else it would not be a first cause. Moreover, if the first cause exists in virtue of its own nature, it will never cease to exist, for it always has its nature, in addition to which it needs nothing at all to make it exist. Therefore, the first cause will never cease to be; and since it has neither beginning nor end, it is eternal.

Since everything in the universe, with the exception of the first cause, had to begin to exist, there was a time when they did not exist. There was a time when the first cause existed all alone. Therefore, when the first cause began to make other things exist, at least the first things were made out of nothing. They began to exist simply because the first cause willed that they should exist. But if the first cause could make one thing out of nothing, it could make any other thing out of nothing. It could, in short, make anything it wished to make. There is only one word that will describe such unlimited power, and that word is *Infinite!*

God is that first cause, a being uncreated, the cause of all other causes, eternal, infinite, and existing separately and independently from the universe.

The Proof from Motion

To most people, the term "motion" immediately conveys the idea of an object like an automobile, a train, a boat, or an airplane, moving from one place to another. However, in developing a proof for the existence of God from the evidence of "motion" in the world, we are using the term in its widest sense. *Motion* applies to the exercise of any activity, internal or external, bodily or spiritual, by any finite being, living or nonliving. In this sense there is motion in the growing of a plant or a tree; in the thinking, willing, or talking of a man as well as in his walking. Motion is the transition from potency to act. Thus, water is potentially hydrogen and oxygen or conversely, hydrogen and oxygen in the right amounts are potentially water. In either case the crossing over from potency to act is motion.

The proof from motion is based on the assumption that there *is* motion in the world and upon the further assumption that whatever is moved is moved by something other than itself. The first assumption is a matter of everyday experience; we observe that things do move. The second assumption has all the force of a law of nature, namely: *whatever is moved is moved by something other than itself*. This means that nothing in the visible world can move entirely of itself, without some outside help. Similarly, no moving thing contains within itself the complete explanation for its movement. Its motion is never self-originating. This law of movement has no exceptions. In the case of lifeless matter, which is inert and cannot move itself, it is easy to understand how this law applies. But in the case of living things, which in a sense "move themselves," it is not immediately apparent.

Let us consider in the first instance the movement of nonliving bodies. They move only as they are moved. They do not move themselves in any way. They get all their motion from without. For example, the steam locomotive: at first sight it seems to be a self-contained mechanism. Fill it up with water and fuel and light the fire and soon it will propel itself along the rails. But does it really move itself? Actually the locomotive is moved by steam, which drives the pistons back and forth to move the rods that move the wheels. But the steam derives its reality and power from the action of fire upon water. Fire and water depend for their force upon their constituent elements and these depend in turn upon other things, and ultimately upon a *first* mover which moves all things. That first mover we call God.

Next, let us consider the movement of the earth on its axis and its motion around the sun, which we know to be proved facts. How did the earth get its motion? Some scientists say that the earth got its motion from the sun, which, while spinning around, flung off our earth as a fragment into space. But from whence did the sun get its motion? Some scientists theorize that the sun got its motion from a large, fiery, whirling nebula, of which it was once a part. Other scientists say that the sun with its motion is the result of a collision between two stars. As to how the motion of the fiery nebula or the stars originated, scientists, up to the present at least, have given us no positive answer. But no matter how far back we trace the motion of the earth, the final answer will reveal that all motion is ultimately due to some unmoved source of motion, which we call the *first mover.* To answer the question as to the source of motion satisfactorily, this first mover must not be moved by any other. There must exist a being above and beyond and distinct from the world who ultimately gave it motion. This is the first mover, God.

Finally, let us consider the motion of living things. In a certain sense, living things move themselves, but they can do so only by receiving help from outside. No living thing gives itself life or the power of self-motion. A plant grows by reason of the energy it receives from the sun and the food it draws from the soil. There is a similar situation in regard to men and animals, insofar as all energy is drawn from the food that is consumed. Also, no living thing preserves itself in being and in activity. Its being and its motion depend ultimately upon the first cause which is also the first mover.

Wherever we find motion, we find that it is stimulated by something other than the thing which is moved. Thus, a man's senses perceive objects, but there must be objects there to perceive, else the senses are not stirred or moved to activity. A man's mind understands truths, but understanding depends on sense knowledge for its beginnings, and sense knowledge depends upon external objects of sensation. Thus neither sensation nor understanding are self-originating, but both are dependent upon an inner life principle which did not make itself, and upon objects of knowledge which did not make themselves. And so it is with all man's activities: the movement to action is caused by something other than the act itself.

Now, if everything moved requires a mover, it is obvious that there must be a beginning to the chain of motion. An infinite series of movers is unthinkable. There must be a *first mover* which is not moved by anything else, namely, a first mover itself unmoved. This first mover is God.

The Proof from Dependence

If anything exists for a time only; or if existence does not belong to its very nature and it is subject to change or destruction; or if we must look beyond it for the reason of its existence, then we say that thing is *dependent*. Anything that is dependent or contingent is so called because it looks to something outside itself for its very existence and continuance in existence.

Actually, everything in the world is dependent because everything in the world is subject to change or decay or death. All living things, plants, animals, and men, come into existence at a given moment, and in a comparatively short time die and pass out of existence. Nonliving things are also constantly undergoing changes, or breaking down into component parts, or combining with other materials to make new substances which in turn will break down into component parts.

Obviously all of these things, living and nonliving, are

dependent. In fact nothing with which we have contact, and no particular thing in the whole visible universe, has any claim on existence. Everything in the universe is dependent, that is, it does not exist of itself, but depends on something else for its existence.

Since the visible world with all that it contains is dependent, it must be held in existence by some being distinct from it. This being is an independent or necessary being who is self-existent, a being to whose nature existence belongs. Such a self-existent being must be able to support in existence all things in the world, including living plants, sentient animals and rational man. This self-existent being must be a living power. He must be the Supreme Being who holds within Himself the source of His own existence. We call Him God.

Similarity in proofs. It must be admitted that there is similarity and some overlapping and repetition between the proofs from Causality, Motion and Dependence. But the point of view in each of the proofs is different. Although each proof leads to the same conclusion, namely, that God exists, each proof throws the searchlight of enquiry upon a different attribute of God. Thus the proof from Causality shows that God is not produced by any other being but is self-existent. The proof from Motion shows that God is not moved by any other being, but is immutable. The proof from Dependence shows that God exists necessarily and without the help of any other being.

The Proof from History

Abraham Lincoln has been credited with a very shrewd observation which reads like this: "You may fool all the people some of the time; you can even fool some of the people all the time; but you can't fool all the people all the time."[1] Upon this type of reasoning is based the proof for the existence of God as drawn from history. History testifies that belief in a Supreme

[1] Quoted in Alexander K. McClure, *Lincoln's Yarns and Stories,* p. 124.

Being has always and everywhere been the universal conviction of mankind. Back as far as we can trace in the history of mankind, men of every race and every condition of culture, civilized and uncivilized, have believed in some supreme being to whom reverence and honor was due. When this belief is examined, tested, and weighed in the balance, it is evident that no other common belief of mankind has been comparably accepted.

Thus it is a belief that has constantly been held by men despite the fact that they would be free from certain duties and obligations and would be more able to do as they wished, if they did not hold it. Those who believe in God and live according to their belief, live useful lives and find happiness and contentment therein. On the contrary, denial of God's existence has never made anyone morally better or contributed in any way to the real happiness of the human race. Although this belief in God has been questioned and tested in every conceivable way, no sensible and solid argument has been produced against it. It has withstood successfully every challenge down through the ages. Furthermore, we cannot believe that man's reason fails him in a matter of such importance. For the question as to whether God exists or does not exist is of vital importance to man both for this life and for the next. Although the conviction of any one man, or even a group of men, might possibly be wrong, the conviction reached by the best intellects of every age and race can hardly be wrong.

The universal belief of mankind in the existence of a Supreme Being is surrounded by such circumstances that it seems not only improbable, but also impossible, that the belief be not true. Therefore, this universal conviction of mankind, considered with all its circumstances, is a convincing proof of the existence of God.

REVIEW QUESTIONS

1 What is an efficient cause? Give an example.
2 What do you mean by an *effect*? Give an example.

3. Is it possible for an effect to contain its cause? Explain.
4. Why is an infinite series of causes unthinkable?
5. What is the First Cause, and why must it be infinite?
6. Why, at least in the beginning, must the First Cause have created out of nothing?
7. Define *motion* in the broad sense in which it is used in apologetics.
8. What are the two facts upon which the argument for the existence of God from motion is constructed?
9. In what sense can a tree be said to be in motion and upon what does this motion depend?
10. In what sense can there be motion in a man's mind and upon what does this motion depend?
11. Why is it necessary to have a first mover and how do we show that this first mover is God?
12. What is meant by saying that something is dependent?
13. How do we reason from a dependent being to the necessity for an independent or self-existent being?
14. Quote Abraham Lincoln's aphorism about "fooling the people." What is it intended to illustrate?
15. How can a universal belief of mankind be used as an argument to prove that God exists?

SUGGESTIONS FOR READING

"The Metaphysical Argument," *Truths Men Live By,* John A. O'Brien. New York: The Macmillan Company, 1956, Chapter XI, pp. 83–95. (Proof for the existence of God as a Necessary Being, since everything we observe about us is contingent, that is, does not necessarily exist.)

"Universal Belief of Mankind," *Ibid.*, Chapter X, pp. 75–83. (The fact that men always and everywhere believe in a Supreme Being is used to prove the existence of God.)

"Arguments for the Existence of God," *Truths to Live By,* J. Elliot Ross, C.S.P. New York: Henry Holt and Company, 1929, Chapter III, pp. 81–115. (Proofs for the existence of God based upon: the impossibility of an infinite series of dependent causes; contingent beings imply a Necessary Being; conscience points to a Supreme Being; the blankness of life without God.)

Baltimore and Ohio Railroad photo

The *diesel-electric train* pictured above appears to be a self-contained mechanism moving itself. Fuel oil is used to operate diesel engines which, in turn, operate dynamos. These dynamos generate electricity, which drives the wheels of the locomotive. This is not, however, the complete story. The train would not move were it not for the fact that oil ignites at a certain temperature and generates gas that expands with great force sufficient to drive pistons back and forth. Furthermore, oil in its crude state was formed in the bowels of the earth through the operation of geological forces extending back ages and ages. Even there the story of motion does not stop until it reaches the first mover, God. Ultimately, then, God is the *first mover* of even the most modern diesel-electric train.

Chapter 4

What we know about God

Existence of God

WE KNOW THAT GOD exists. We proved this in the preceding chapters by several arguments from reason. However, it is one thing to know that God exists, but it is quite another matter to know something about the nature of God. Apologetics is chiefly concerned with showing that God exists. Consideration of the nature and attributes of God is more the province of philosophy and theology than of apologetics, but apologetics is definitely interested in showing what sort of relationship exists between God and man. The fact that God created man establishes this as a relationship of dependency. But this dependency will become more real and vivid to us as we increase our knowledge of both God and man.

Limitations on Our Knowledge

There are definite limitations on the knowledge we can acquire about God through our unaided reason. Nevertheless, the attainment of such knowledge as is possible with unaided reason is the task which we undertake. Let us be warned at the outset, we who have the gift of faith, that the conception of God which we obtain from unaided reason must needs be cold and formal. Without revelation and without the warm, human personality of Christ to interpret God the Creator for us, the knowledge we acquire will be far from satisfying to one illumined by faith.

This does not mean, of course, that revelation and faith open the way to a complete knowledge of God. Even with revelation and faith our knowledge is limited. This is so chiefly because of the greatness of God and the smallness of our minds. Also, we are not able to apprehend God directly, because our senses and intellect are not suited for this. We must rise with an effort from material things through created beings to the uncreated, infinite spirit who is God.

How We Attain Knowledge

Our knowledge of God comes to us piecemeal, pretty much as we acquire knowledge of anything that we find difficult to comprehend. In the case of God, however, our puny reason will never be able to comprehend fully One who is so far superior to us. Nevertheless, we get some ideas about the nature of God from our consideration of the proofs for God's existence. Also, acting on the principle that we can know something about the nature of a cause from the nature of its effects, we get other notions about God by referring to Him in an unlimited way the perfections we observe in creatures. At the same time we remove from our idea of God all the imperfections we observe in creatures. In doing this we realize that there is no real division or distinction of perfections in God because, in some incomprehensible way, all perfections are identical with His nature or essence. Nevertheless, with all its limitations, such knowledge as we acquire through reason will give us a better appreciation and understanding of God.

God's Attributes

We know, of course, that God is a pure Spirit, that is, He is not composed of parts united together as in a material being, otherwise He could not be the First Cause. We also know that God created the universe out of nothingness and that everything has received its existence from Him. Had we reasoned more deeply about this truth we would see that God is Existence itself. He is the Master of Existence. He can give existence to anything that can conceivably exist. Consequently, not only must He possess every perfection that can conceivably exist, but He possesses it in the highest degree. Therefore we say that God is infinite.

We note, for example, that God's creature, man, can know and act justly and be wise, good and merciful. These perfections, although limited in man, imply no imperfections in themselves. We reason, therefore, that such perfections must be found in God in an infinite way. We say that God is all-knowing, all-just, all-wise, all-good, all-merciful. But when we note that man is possessed, for example, of the virtue of courage, we do not apply this to God and say that He is all-courageous. Courage implies that one can overcome dangers or difficulties without giving way to cowardice or fear, and clearly this would not apply to the infinite, all-powerful God. Likewise we remove from our idea of God the imperfections which we observe in material things. Every material thing is finite: it had a beginning, it does not exist necessarily, and it will not always exist. But God is infinite, a necessary Being, eternal, without beginning or end.

As a by-product of our reasoning about the arguments for God's existence, we came to know some of His other attributes. These proofs not only convince us that God exists but they also tell us much about His nature. Thus when we proved that God is the Supreme Designer and Creator of the universe we realized that He must be possessed of infinite intelligence, wisdom and power. When we reasoned about the wonderful order that exists in the universe, and particularly about how all things work out for the best interests of God's creatures, we found out about God's Providence. We came to realize, also, that in creating the universe God had a definite purpose, because an intelligent being must always have a purpose in acting.

God's Purpose in Creation

Wherever there is intelligence, wherever there is design, there is purpose. "A review of the wonders of nature," writes the scientist, A. C. Morrison, "demonstrates beyond question that there are design and purpose in it all. A program is being carried out in all its infinite detail by the Supreme Being we call God" (Revell, *Man Does Not Stand Alone*, 1947, p. 95).

Through the process of reasoning we can discover God's purpose in creating the world. God is absolutely self-sufficient. He needs nothing for His own happiness but Himself. Although He did create the universe, neither the universe nor man is necessary to Him. He did not create the universe for creatures directly because they did not exist when the universe was created. Therefore the purpose in creation cannot be found in creatures themselves but must lie wholly in God. The only assignable reason for creation, therefore, is that God, who is *infinite goodness*, willed to communicate being to creatures in order that they might share in His infinite being, goodness and happiness. But only free and intelligent creatures, who see the glory and goodness of God, could come to know Him, freely offer Him honor, praise and love, and thereby attain their own happiness.

A Personal God

If God, in creating the world, intended the happiness of His creatures as one of His purposes He could not be an impersonal Being, far removed from His creatures. He could not be merely "an aloof and mysterious force" behind the universe, an "eternal energy," that somehow is intended to explain the existence of things. He must be a God who has a personal interest in all His creatures in a way similar to the interest which a father of a family has in his children. We call this belief in a *personal* God. To man especially has God evidenced this personal care and affection. This becomes very apparent when you compare man with other creatures. Man alone of all God's creatures on earth was chosen to share God's happiness through knowing, loving and serving Him. Hence God gave man an intellect or reasoning faculty so that he might know Him and a faculty of free will so that he might freely love and serve Him. No other creature on earth has thus been distinguished and set apart by God. It should be evident that God must love all men individually, since He has given to all these same faculties for knowing, loving, and serving Him. In the light of God's fatherly solicitude for men, it would be most unreasonable for anyone to doubt that there is a personal bond of affection between God and himself.

God's Providence

Not only did God have a purpose in creating the universe, but in His infinite wisdom and power He sees to it that this purpose is continuously carried out. The ways and means that God uses to accomplish this we call the *providence* of God (Example 7). We saw examples of this providence when we were engaged in proving that God is the Supreme Lawgiver who impresses upon all things in nature the laws to govern their activities and who makes known His moral law to man and speaks individually to him through the voice of conscience. All of this is meant when we talk about the providence of God. But let us put first things first.

If God's purpose in creating the world is to be accomplished, His providence will see to it that all things necessary to His plan will be kept in existence until their purpose is fulfilled. Nothing can exist, nothing can act without the continual help of God. If at any moment God were to withdraw His support everything would return to the nothingness from which it came. This is but a reasonable deduction from what we know of creation. If creatures have no power to bring themselves into existence, neither have they power to keep themselves in existence. God who willed that they begin to exist must also will that they continue to exist.

Existence is only the first result of God's providence. In order that existing things may serve the purpose for which God wished them to exist, everything in the world must live up to the laws established by the Creator. In His providence God has created a law for everything, and it is through the knowledge of these laws that man is able to reason back to the existence of a Supreme Lawgiver as we did in a previous chapter of this book.

The laws which God established to govern the universe fall into two classifications. There are the physical laws which govern in a general way everything created, but which are particularly binding on all creatures not possessed of reason. These physical laws affect man insofar as he has a material body, but in many instances he can ignore them at his own peril. These physical laws bind nonintelligent creatures, living or nonliving, in such a way that they are forced to act in accordance with God's purpose in creating them. Thus an animal acts as it does instinctively and its life in general is governed by strong instinctive tendencies which cannot be resisted.

But for His favored creature, man, the only creature on earth possessed of intelligence and free will, God established the moral law. God does not force man to obey the moral law. Instead He gave man the gift of intelligence to understand God's purpose in creating the world, to recognize man's relationship of dependence on God, and to be able to distinguish between good and evil. God also gave man the gift of free will; he could obey the law or not, and choose good or evil. It is reasonable to believe that God, having given man free will, will not interfere with that free will even though man is disposed to disobey the moral law. At the same time it is also reasonable to think that God will give man strong motives for observing the law. Therefore, we conclude that in God's providence there must be a system of rewards and punishments.

Example 7. *God's Intelligence, Wisdom and Providence Evident in Physical Laws.* "Water is really the life-blood of our earth, yet we accept its rhythmical migration from sea to sky, and from sky to sea again, as lightly as we do the circulation of the vital fluid through our veins. How wonderfully perfect is the process of evaporation, forever going on from all the lakes and oceans of our globe, as from these mighty reservoirs the solar heat draws moisture upward in the form of vapour! For water, being many hundred times heavier than air, could in no other form be lifted several miles above the earth. Yet this supply, prodigious though it be, floats lightly in the empyrean in the shape of clouds,—huge, sunlit galleons, filled with precious cargoes, waiting patiently to be unloaded. These vaporous ships are filled and emptied without human hands; and sail to their respective ports without a helmsman, chart or compass. Currents in air, like currents in the sea, convey them far into the heart of continents, that they may there discharge their freights over the very fields in which stand waiting husbandmen. The total quantity of water thus delivered in rain or snow is inconceivable. Sometimes a single cloud contains thousands of tons of liquid, which, if released at once would sweep away both vegetation and the soil itself; yet with what delicate precision is its distribution usually effected! True, cloudbursts do sometimes occur, as if to remind man what might always be the case, but for the care of Providence; yet as a rule, nothing can be more gentle than the fall of moisture to the earth. The rain sifts through the atmosphere in billions of small drops, as if poured through a finely woven sieve, alighting from a dizzy height without the crushing of a leaf or flower; and on its way cleans the air of its impurities, as later on, in the form of rivers, it will sweep them to the sea" (Stoddard, *Rebuilding a Lost Faith*, pp. 36–37).

Man Indebted to God

The consideration of what reason can tell us about God should help us to grasp more clearly our relationship of dependence upon God. It is to be hoped that this relationship will not appear overly cold and formal by contrast with the God whom we know by faith and through the person of Jesus Christ. Until such time as God manifests Himself to those who faithfully make use of their reason to know Him, and of their wills to love and serve Him, we must be satisfied with such knowledge of God as our finite minds can laboriously acquire. Unfortunately, at this stage of our apologetic reasoning we can have no recourse to revelation and to the warm personal knowledge of God that comes to us by way of Bethlehem and Calvary.

However, continued reflection on the truths thus far established from reason should lead to such convictions as the following: God by His own choice has created the universe. Moreover, every good thing that we possess, our life and our very being, all have been given to us by God, who holds us in existence from one moment to the next. Without God's supporting hand we, and the whole world with us, would lapse into the nothingness from which He originally called us. Therefore, while the infinite wisdom and power of God overawe us, His supreme goodness prompts us to adore Him and to love Him with our whole heart and mind and soul. It is probable that this sentiment will be strengthened and reinforced when we have considered a little more fully what we know of man, and prove, as we intend to do in the following chapter, that God has given to man a spiritual and immortal soul.

REVIEW QUESTIONS

1 Why can we not perceive God directly?
2 In what way do we obtain knowledge about God through reason?
3 If, in addition to reason, we have revelation and faith to guide us, would this remove all limitation on our knowledge of God?
4 How do we know that God is a pure Spirit?
5 What do you mean by *infinite?*
6 How do we know that God is infinite?
7 Why do we say that God must have had a purpose in creating the universe?
8 Can we discover God's purpose in creating the universe?
9 Why do we use the adjective *personal* before the name *God?*
10 What do you mean by God's providence?
11 How does the idea of reward and punishment derive from a rational conception of God's providence?
12 How can the knowledge of God made known by reason thus far, be used to awaken sentiments of love and gratitude toward Him?

SUGGESTIONS FOR READING

"Christ Manifests God," *Truths Men Live By*, John A. O'Brien. New York: The Macmillan Company, 1946. Chapter XII, pp. 95–101.

"The Nature of God and His Relations to His Creatures," *Truths to Live By*, J. Elliot Ross. New York: Henry Holt and Company, 1929. Chapter IV, pp. 117–155.

"The Nature of God," *Ibid.*, Chapter XIII, pp. 101–126. (Discusses God's attributes. Also shows that human freedom can be reconciled with God's knowledge.)

A Description of God, Richard Ginder. The Catholic Information Society, 214 West 31st Street, New York 1, N.Y. 16 pp., 5¢. (His attributes, etc.)

What's God Like? Richard Ginder. The Catholic Information Society. 14 pp., 5¢. (Discusses the infinite intelligence and wisdom of God.)

Max Tharpe photo

"How wonderfully perfect is the process of evaporation, forever going on from all the lakes and oceans of our globe . . . . this supply, prodigious though it be, floats lightly in the empyrean in the shape of clouds,—huge, sunlit galleons, filled with precious cargoes, waiting patiently to be unloaded . . . *over the very fields in which stand waiting husbandmen.*"

Chapter 5

What we know about man

Man, a Living Being

THE TRUTH OF MAN'S existence as a living, reasoning (human) being we take to be self-evident. We assume also that it is evident that man's existence on this earth is limited. The life on earth of any individual man begins with birth and ends with death. Man is not a self-existent being nor can he be said to be the cause of his own existence. In fact we have used man's body with its marvelous organs and physical and spiritual powers as evidence that there is a Supreme Being who is God, the Creator of the universe.

Man's dominion over plant and animal life. Although man did not originate or create plant and animal life, he is clearly and unquestionably the ruler of all living things on this earth. For the most part, man is able to grow the grains, fruit, and vegetables that he wishes for food. Even where nature does not supply proper soil or sufficient moisture for growing things, by using his reason and inventiveness man can largely supply for this deficiency through artificial irrigation and fertilizers. Although animals excel man in many ways—in sense perception, in strength, agility and rapidity of motion—man is easily their master. For example, the horse, the elephant, the ox, and the mule greatly exceed man in strength; nevertheless man has adapted these animals as his beasts of burden. Although ferocious animals like the lion and the tiger have a more acute sense of smell, more highly sensitive hearing, greater depth and sharpness of vision, and are more swift and silent in motion than man, they are no match for man, who through his intelligence can capture them alive and cage them. But you never hear of animals thus trapping men!

The Source of Man's Superiority

The explanation for man's superiority over plant and animal life is not hard to find. Plants have life and the power to grow and to put forth leaf and flower in proper season. Animals also have life and the power of growth, but unlike plants they have sensation, that is, they can feel pain or pleasure, and they possess freedom of motion. But man, who has the power of growth like the plant and the feeling and freedom of movement like the animal, has in addition the powers of reasoning and of making a free choice. It is this ability to reason and to exercise free choice which gives man superiority over all living things on this earth.

Man's reason. As does the lower animal, man gets his knowledge of material things through the senses of sight, hearing, smell, touch, and taste. But man is able to take the information which the senses give him, classify, order, and arrange it, and make general judgments or even arrive at new information. This is the power of reasoning. It is because man has this ability to reason that he has been able to make such remarkable progress in all his undertakings. A nonreasoning creature, no matter how skilled by nature in doing things, is perpetually at a standstill and never makes any progress.

Man's power of choice. In addition, man has the ability to choose freely between two or more ways of acting, whereas a nonreasoning creature in acting is directed invariably by his instinct. This is the power of free will. It is because man has this gift of free will that his work is marked by diversity, while the work of nonreasoning creatures is characterized by uniformity and does not change because the creature does not have free will.

Man's soul. Now every living thing has within itself the source of its own special powers. We call that source the *principle of life*[1] in plants and animals, and the *soul* in man. It is this soul in man which gives him his special distinction and sharply differentiates him from plants and animals. The more that apologetics can know about man's soul through reason, the more will be clarified the relationship between God the Creator and man the creature.

Now no one has ever actually seen the soul in man just as no one has ever seen God the Creator. But we can know God through His works. In a similar way, we can learn something about man's soul by observing what it enables him to do. In studying the nature of what man is able to accomplish through his powers of intellect (ability to think or reason) and free will (ability to do or not to do), we will be able to demonstrate that man has a soul which is both spiritual and immortal. As a by-product of this study we should be able to appreciate more

[1] Sometimes *soul* is used to designate the vital principle of plants and animals, but this is not the common usage. In such a case reference is made to a material soul, not a spiritual soul.

fully how greatly God has blessed man by conferring on him these marvelous gifts of intellect and free will.

Man's Soul Is Spiritual

We have already explained that the soul is the principle of life in man and, as such, is the source of his ability to live and to move and to exercise his senses as well as his own special powers of intellect and will. By the term *spiritual* we describe a living substance that is simple and not composed of parts, something that is immaterial.

In developing our proofs for the existence of a spiritual soul in man we will rely on the principle that every effect must have a proportionate cause and that the effect will tell us something of the cause that produced it. Thus there must be some adequate cause in man for the things which we see men do.

The role of the senses. As a creature of flesh and blood man is equipped by nature to know only material things. Knowledge of these material things reaches man's brain through the channels of his five senses. Some material things can be known by only one sense; for example, the sound of a recording of a symphony orchestra. Other material things can be known by two or more senses simultaneously, for example, the sight, smell, and touch of a bouquet of roses. But, being material, man's senses cannot of themselves go beyond what is material. They cannot apprehend directly anything that is immaterial.

"Man is like a city with five gates through each of which messengers come with tidings of what is passing in the outer world. These gates are the five senses, and each sense allows some special kind of knowledge to pass in. Man has no other means than these of knowing anything about the external world. Through the eye he gets a knowledge of color, through the ear of sound, through the nose of smell, through the palate of taste, and through the whole surface of the body, but particularly through the hands, he comes to know of the resistance, hardness, and softness of bodies and such like.

"The eye is the organ, or instrument, of sight, the ear of hearing, and so with the rest. Each organ is a part of the body, or, for the sense of touch, the entire body, and is acted on only by things that are themselves bodies—that is, by things that are material, things that have length, breadth, and thickness. The eye cannot see an object, unless its retina be set in motion by the vibrating ether; the ear cannot hear a sound, unless its tympanum be struck by the air waves; the nostrils cannot perceive the perfume of a flower, unless the minute fragrant particles actually penetrate to them; the palate cannot taste, the hand cannot feel without coming into direct contact with their objects" (Sheehan, *Apologetics and Catholic Doctrine,* p. 51).

Man's ability to know immaterial things. However, man does come to know things that cannot be perceived by the senses, for example, such abstract ideas as virtue, patriotism, piety and so on. These are called *immaterial* things because although real, they cannot be seen, touched, heard, tasted or smelled. Patriotism, for example, is not tangible to any of the senses. Yet one can have such a definite idea of patriotism that he does not hesitate to assert its presence or absence in a given individual because such a one either measures up to or does not measure up to the idea of patriotism existing in the mind.

Man also has ideas about real spiritual beings, like God and angels, which are above and beyond the reach of his senses. Since man is able to know these immaterial and spiritual things he must have within him another faculty which is immaterial or spiritual. The effect must tell us at least this much about the cause. You cannot get blood out of a stone! Neither can you expect to get something immaterial or spiritual from a purely material source. We are forced to conclude that there is something in man which is immaterial or spiritual. This we call man's soul.

Man's ability to reason. Man is able to take the information which his senses convey to him, think about it, and from different objects presented to him to distill one type of information in order to form the abstract ideas we mentioned above. Man is also able to take truths already known and by thinking about them to infer or deduce some new truth. This is what is meant by reasoning. It is an ability which cannot be attributed to man's senses nor to his brain nor to any material cause because it is an immaterial act on the part of man and must have an immaterial cause. We therefore infer that there must be something in man that is immaterial or spiritual. This immaterial something is man's spiritual soul.

This ability of man to *reason* about things is responsible for the marvelous inventions and progress which man has made down through the centuries. All the improvements which have taken place in the past, all the improvements which we witness in the present, have come about because man is able to reason.

In sharp contrast to this is the situation of the lower animals. Because they cannot think or reason, animals never make any improvements or any progress in their way of doing things. Some animals have been gifted by nature with marvelous abilities which are instinctive but their instincts cause them to perform the same actions century after century without changes or improvements. Witness, for example, the spider and his web, or the honeybee and the honeycomb.

Man's free will. Finally, man has the gift of *free will*. He has the power of choice. Confronted with two alternatives, he can choose this one or that one. Also, man can make a decision that he will perform a certain act. Thus he may resolve to make an act of thanksgiving to God for blessings received. In so doing he recognizes the existence of God who cannot be seen, heard, felt, or touched. He knows that he is indebted to the invisible God for His blessings. Then he makes an act of will, which is also invisible and immaterial. All these acts are spiritual and not material, consequently they prove the existence of something in man which is likewise spiritual and not material.

Man's ability to reason, to form abstract ideas, to arrive at new truths from old truths, and to exercise free will, are all immaterial acts. In accordance with the truth that every effect must have an adequate cause, these acts prove that man has within him an immaterial principle which can be responsible for these immaterial acts. We call this immaterial principle in man the *soul.* We say that this soul is *spiritual* to indicate that it is a living thing which has activities that are not material and to distinguish it from the principle of life in animals.

Man's Soul Is Immortal

To be immortal means to be imperishable, that is, not subject to death. When we apply this term to man's soul it means that, once created by God, the soul will live on forever. This belief in immortality in one form or another has been the universal belief of men from the earliest times. There are those, of course, who deny the existence of a spiritual soul and immortality and there are others who do not reject the belief in immortality but claim that it cannot be proved by arguments based on reason.

We claim that the immortality of the soul can be proved from reason by (1) the argument from the nature of the soul, (2) the argument from the desire of man for perfect happiness, and (3) the argument from the demands of justice.

The argument from the nature of the soul. The soul has no *need* to die at the separation of body and soul because God has created it as a distinct thing. It was created to be united with the body and, in its activities, to use the assistance of the body. But the fact that it uses the body does not prove that it cannot exist without the body. The pianist who cannot produce his music without the piano is separate from, and can exist without the piano. The body, composed as it is of chemical elements, cannot be the reason for the existence of the soul which is immaterial and spiritual.

When an animal dies, its soul or vital principle ceases to

exist, for, insofar as it is inseparably united to the body, it is material. With man it is different, for his soul is spiritual and has activities—thinking and willing—for which a body is not essential. It should be evident, therefore, that *the soul of man does not need to cease to exist just because it is separated from the body.*

Moreover, death, which is the separation of the soul from the body, has no effect upon the existence of the soul. The body, which is material, breaks up into its constituent parts. But the soul is spiritual or immaterial and is not made up of parts. There is no reason to believe, therefore, that man's soul will cease to exist upon leaving the body at death.

The argument from the desire for happiness. Back of all man's strivings there is the desire, under one guise or another, for perfect and permanent happiness. The attainment of this happiness, in some form or other, is the underlying motive for everything that man does. So universally true is this of all men without exception that it is only reasonable to conclude that the desire for perfect happiness is rooted in the very nature of man. Experience teaches that perfect happiness is not obtainable in this life. If the truth of this statement is not immediately evident a little reflection should convince anyone. Even when a man has everything that this world can offer—honor, wealth, power—and seems to enjoy everything in full measure, the realization that sooner or later all this must end is a preventative of perfect happiness. Death will ultimately strip one of every earthly possession.

Since, therefore, the desire for this perfect happiness is rooted in the nature of man, and God is the author of this nature, reason tells us that God, who created such a desire in human nature, must also have created the possibility of fulfilling that desire. If the desire cannot be fully satisfied in this life then God must allow the souls of the just, at least, to live on after the death of the body, so that perfect happiness may be obtained and man's desire be fulfilled. Otherwise God would be cruelly tantalizing men by creating in them a strong desire for perfect happiness with no possible means of fulfillment. This of course would contradict what we know of the goodness and mercy of God.

The argument from the demands of justice. Almost from daily experience we know that the strict demands of justice are frequently not realized in this life. Very often evil men prosper while good men suffer misfortunes. Now we know that God, the judge of our merits, is infinitely just. If, therefore, virtue is not always rewarded in this life nor vice punished, it is only reasonable to believe that there is another life beyond the grave in which the justice of God will triumph. In order that the inequalities of this life may be set straight, the good rewarded and the evil punished, immortality of the soul seems to be indicated.

Other Characteristics of Man's Soul

Each soul separately created. Purely material things cannot produce immaterial results. This is of the very nature of things. The human body, which is material, is formed in the body of the mother, which is also material. It is not possible that the material body of the mother could produce the immaterial soul. Therefore on reasonable grounds we hold that each human soul is individually created by God.

INDIVIDUAL. A man's soul is his own, that is, it is independent of other souls. We are conscious of this fact. You know that the soul which acts within you is *your* soul, not anybody else's.

PERMANENT. You are conscious that you are the same person that you were ten or more years ago although your body has undergone changes and, as scientists tell us, is completely renewed about every seven years. The fact that you recognize and accept as *your* acts things which you did years and years ago proves that your soul is permanent and that one and the same soul has resided in you all that time.

Man's Debt of Gratitude to God

It is a salutary thing for man to know that he owes his existence to the creative act of God. This knowledge establishes definitely the relationship of dependency that exists between God and man. But it is only when one attempts to answer the question, "What is Man?" that the full significance of this relationship between God and man is made clear. When we prove from reason that man has a spiritual and immortal soul with all the marvelous powers and prerogatives that go with it, we can understand more clearly what it means when we say that God is a personal God who has a personal care for each one of His children.

God has lavished on man the ability to think and to reason, the great gift and personal responsibility of free will, and an immortal soul which is destined to enjoy Him for all eternity. The natural reaction ought to be, "What shall I render to the Lord for all that He has rendered to me?" A partial answer to this question will be given in the following chapter when we seek to prove that man has an obligation to practice religion.

REVIEW QUESTIONS

1. In what way can man be said to be the ruler of all living things on earth?
2. What connection is there between man's spiritual soul and his material progress?
3. What makes man a living being?
4. What difference is there between the principle of life in animals and men?
5. What is meant by an immaterial thing?
6. What is meant by a spiritual substance and how does this differ from an immaterial substance?
7. Give reasons why you agree or disagree with the following statement: "Every spirit is immaterial but not every immaterial thing is a spirit."
8. What is meant by saying that every effect must have a proportionate cause?

9 What is meant by saying that an effect will tell us something of the cause that produced it?
10 What part do the senses play in man's intellectual life?
11 What ability is required to develop new truths from old truths?
12 Give examples of something material perceivable by (a) only one sense, and (b) by the five senses.
13 Give three examples of immaterial ideas, with an explanation for each.
14 What is remarkable about the idea of patriotism?
15 In what sense is an act of the will invisible and immaterial?
16 What does *immortal* mean?
17 Why can the soul of man live on after the body?
18 What has the desire for happiness to do with immortality?
19 What has the demand for justice to do with immortality?
20 What gives man a sense of continuity (the conviction that he is identically the same person that he was a dozen or more years ago)?
21 How do we know from reason that the soul is individually created?

SUGGESTIONS FOR READING

"The Freedom of the Will," *Truths Men Live By,* John A. O'Brien. New York: The Macmillan Company, 1946, chapter XXIV, pp. 247–270.

"Immortality," *Rebuilding a Lost Faith,* John L. Stoddard. New York: P. J. Kenedy & Sons, 1924, chapter VI, pp. 52–63.

Life Without End, Richard Ginder. The Catholic Information Society, 214 West 31st Street, New York 1, N.Y. 16 pp., 5¢.

Man: Worth 73¢ or Billions? John A. O'Brien. The Catholic Information Society. 14 pp., 5¢. (Man's physical body has very little intrinsic worth. It is the spiritual soul that gives man his priceless value.)

Shall We Live Again? John A. O'Brien. The Paulist Press, 401 West 59th Street, New York 19, N.Y., 1946. 32 pp., 10¢. (Reprint of Chapter XXV, *Truths Men Live By,* "The Immortality of the Soul.")

The Soul, What Is It? John A. O'Brien. The Paulist Press. 32 pp., 10¢. (Reprint of Chapters XXI, XXII, XXIII, of *Truths Men Live By.* "God's Image in Man," "The Soul: Substantial and Simple," and "The Spirituality of the Soul.")

The Anti-Immortals, L. Rumble, M.S.C. Radio Replies Press Society, St. Paul 1, Minnesota. 32 pp., 15¢. (Presents clearly the various arguments for the immortality of the soul.)

Wide World photo

St. Patrick's Cathedral appears here as a huge cross viewed from the thirty-ninth floor of the International Building in Rockefeller Center, New York City. It seems especially fitting that this beautiful Gothic church, a monument to the worship of God, should be set down in the midst of the proud skyscrapers, as if to remind man that his spiritual gifts of intellect and free will, bestowed on him by God, have made it possible for him to erect both cathedral and skyscrapers.

Chapter 6

The worship of God

Man's Relationship to God

EXCEPT FOR HIS intelligent creatures, God sees to it that all creation carries out His plans for the universe automatically and without variation. Nonintelligent creation, whether living or nonliving, is bound to follow the physical laws which God has established. Animals are also compelled to follow the direction of the instincts which God has impressed on their nature. Of all God's earthly creatures, man alone has been left free to give or to withhold compliance with God's purpose in creating him. Through the process of reasoning we have decided that God's purpose in creating the world was for the glory that would come to Him through the praise, honor and love of intelligent creatures. If God is to receive from man this praise, honor and love which are His due, man's intellect must understand his relationship to God and his will must be motivated to give freely this glory to God.

In the preceding chapters we have recognized man's complete dependence upon God not only for his existence but also for his continuation in existence. We have also laid the groundwork for the motivation that will prompt us freely to give glory to God. Thus, in proving the existence of God, we had reason to marvel at His power, magnificence and goodness. He is the infinite and all-powerful creator of the universe and all that is contained therein, including man. As we considered what reason has to tell us about the nature of God we must have been moved by the realization of the personal interest God takes in all His creatures, especially man. We must have been grateful also in the knowledge of God's providence, by which He rules over the universe with wisdom and justice and power. Furthermore, when we considered how extremely generous God has been to man by giving him a spiritual and immortal soul and the unique powers of reasoning and free will, our motivation to give God the praise, honor and love which is due Him should have become stronger and more personal.

The late Archbishop Sheehan described the foundation upon which all religion is built in the following brief but expressive passage: "We have discovered the great fundamental truths that God of His own free will has created the universe; that He has given us every good thing we possess, our life and our very being; that He holds us in existence from instant to instant; that, without His supporting hand, we and the whole world with us would lapse into the nothingness from which He has called us; that He is supreme goodness and power. Our reason casts us at His feet. It impels us to a great act of loving adoration. It bids us tell Him that we love Him with our whole heart and mind and soul, and that we humbly and gladly acknowledge His absolute dominion over us and our absolute dependence on Him" (Sheehan, *Apologetics and Catholic Doctrine*, p. 32).

Man's duty to God. Thus reason tells us that not only must man recognize these truths, but he must also make some return of gratitude to God. No other creature on earth has been so endowed with the intelligence and free will which make it possible for him to know God and to love and serve Him freely. Would it not be most ungrateful if man did not acknowledge in a suitable way God's great love for him?

To be ungrateful is to be unjust, whereas reason demands that we be just toward all. To be just means that we give to everyone what belongs to him. Consequently, we are strictly obligated to give to God the praise, honor and love that belong to Him, the more so in token repayment for all that He has done for us. The practice of religion is man's duty to God.

The Meaning and Purpose of Religion

Religion is the word that is used to designate the composite of attitudes, beliefs, and acts which are involved in this giving to God of that which is due Him. The word itself is derived from the Latin word *religare* which means "to bind back," and signifies the bond that exists between God and man as Creator and creature. Religion means, therefore, the free acceptance by man of his dependence on God and the acknowledgment of this dependence by suitable acts of worship.

It is important to grasp the significance of man's absolute dependence on God for existence. This truth brings sharply to mind man's own nothingness when confronted with the greatness and goodness of God. From this truth springs man's chief duty to love God with his whole heart and soul as the giver of all good gifts and as the sustainer of his very life and being.

Therefore, while this relationship between God and man rests primarily upon dependency, it means much more. God created man to know Him, to love Him and to serve Him in this world that he may be happy with Him forever in the next. In return for giving glory to God man is to have everlasting happiness. Certainly God has been most generous with man in thus rewarding him for that to which he is in duty bound. On his part, man must recognize in God the kind and loving Father who is interested in his welfare and desires his eternal happiness. To this Father man may have recourse in all the joys, sorrows, misfortunes, and perplexities of life. It is the purpose of religion to facilitate this communication with God and to help man to serve God faithfully and to attain the eternal happiness which God has prepared for those who love Him.

The Practice of Religion

Once man has arrived at a knowledge of his real dependence on God and has reasoned out God's plan and purpose in creating him, he should be able to arrive at a threefold conviction of his relationship with God. First, God is, of course, the Supreme Being, the Creator who made him; secondly, God is the benefactor who provides for his happiness; and thirdly, God is a Father who loves him without stint. This is the threefold attitude which man should have toward God and it should be manifest in the following acts of religion. By an *act of recognition* man submits himself in all things to God, his sovereign Master. By an *act of hope* man puts his trust in God, who provides everything in the present and who has promised him future happiness. By an *act of love* man submits himself to God as a Father who loves him, and endeavors to return the filial love of a son for the infinite love of his Father. In fulfilling these commitments to God (subjective religion) it was inevitable that man should develop a body of beliefs and customs which would surround the manifestation of his internal acknowledgment of dependence upon God. This gives to religion an objective character so that it stands forth as something apart from the person who practices religion (objective religion).

The Necessity for Religion

Despite the clarity with which it is possible to see the relationship which exists between Creator and creature, between God and man, there are some men who seem to think that any formal recourse to religion is unnecessary and unprofitable. In the forefront of those who ignore, or even ridicule religion, are of course atheists and agnostics.

The atheist who wants to make his disbelief in the existence of God appear reasonable, frequently attacks religion by ascribing its origin to motives of fear, superstition, or deception. Religion is thus "outmoded," an "anachronism" in an "enlightened age." "Religion is the opiate of the people," as the Russian communistic and godless propaganda expresses it. But the falsity of all these arguments can be readily proved. Religion is the product of reason; it is a part of man's nature; he cannot do without it. It would be just as easy for man to stop reasoning altogether as it would be to get away from religion permanently. This is as true of man today as it was in ages long past because religion has always been based on the same fundamental process of reasoning. Man reasoned then, as man reasons now, from effect to cause until he arrived at a First Cause, or God. If God is the Creator and men are his creatures then a dependency exists between Creator and creatures. The recognition of this dependency in the mind of man is the beginning of religion.

In addition there are thousands of other persons who do not deny the existence of God but seldom or never make any pretense to a formal practice of religion. Never having considered thoughtfully the implications of their relationship with God they see no great importance in the practice of religion. We claim, on the other hand, that both as a duty to his Creator and in his own enlightened self-interest the practice of religion is a necessity for every man. There are several proofs to support this statement.

Religion and justice. To everyone his due! Debts must be paid! Justice must be done! These are statements that spring from the clear concept of justice which is impressed on the mind and heart of man. All right-thinking men are aware of these demands of justice because conscience, the voice of reason, reminds them repeatedly. Now, to whom is man more deeply indebted than to God, his Creator and generous Heavenly Father? Justice must be done! Consequently, to God as Creator and Master, man owes obedience, honor, and respect. To God as a kind and loving Father, man owes love and gratitude. But obedience, honor, respect, love, and gratitude are all acts of religion. It should be clear, therefore, that justice demands religion.

Religion and gratitude. Gratitude is due in justice to God for the many favors received. Certainly there is no one to whom man is more indebted than to God, to whom he owes his creation and continued existence. All man's gifts of mind and body are attributable to God and it is upon His goodness that man depends for happiness. Prompted by the voice of reason, man's inmost sense of justice bids him to be grateful to God for all these favors. The refusal or failure of man to pay this debt of gratitude is most unjust, and no injustice is more keenly felt than that of ingratitude. It is, therefore, only reasonable to expect that, out of gratitude, man will acknowledge the goodness and mercy of God through acts of religion.

Religion and order. Good order contributes to happiness and peace of mind. There is no happiness in disorder. There is an order of precedence in the universe. God, the Creator, comes before all His creatures; man takes precedence over animals and plants; animals, in turn, come before plants; and all living things take precedence over nonliving things. The order in the universe is well-defined. Man is clearly dependent upon God. Therefore, the maintenance of this good order requires, and reason dictates, that man should acknowledge his dependence, recognize that he is inferior to God, and manifest this in all his actions. Good order also requires that finite man submit his judgment to the infinite God in all things. This means that man must be subject to the will of God in everything, regardless of what he himself would like to do. When God commands, man should submit to these commands because they come from One who is infinitely superior to him and infinitely more wise. Now it is through religion that we come to know of God's commandments. Therefore, religion is necessary for us in order that we may know what God commands and how we may conform to His will and thus observe the right order that contributes to peace and happiness of mind.

Good order requires also that honor and respect be given to whomsoever they are rightly due. But God is our highest superior and worthy of the greatest honor and respect that we can give Him. How can we show this honor and respect to the infinite God? Religion has at least a partial answer. Through the prayers and forms of worship of religion man singly or joined in society with others shows honor and respect to God. Reason tells us that religion is therefore necessary in order that man may offer to God the honor and respect that is due Him.

Religion required for man's happiness. Man is always reaching out for happiness. The yearning for happiness is the constant and universal desire of mankind. What constitutes happiness in this life has been a matter of debate among philosophers from the earliest times. Aristotle, the ancient Greek philosopher, has answered this question wisely. He tells us that happiness consists simply in living in accordance with one's nature. Since man's nature is essentially rational, that is, governed by his reasoning power, man must live in accordance with reason in order to be happy. Knowledge of his dependence on God is one of the first and chief things which reason makes known to man. Unless man acknowledges this dependence in some suitable way, in both thought and act, he is not living in accordance with his nature.

Furthermore, God created man to glorify Him, and happiness was to be the reward of man's voluntary service to God. Since that was the intention of God, reason tells us that ultimately God will have His way. To glorify God means to praise, honor and respect God, all acts of religion. Experience proves that anyone having a true knowledge of God and man's dependence upon Him can enjoy no true and lasting happiness, even here below, if he refuses to glorify God through acts of religion.

Religion required by society. God is, indirectly at least, the Author of human society. Thus the community—the State—owes its origin to God, insofar as God implanted in man's nature the necessity of living and working together with others in society. This is necessary for man's perfection and well-being in this life as well as being helpful to him in the attainment of eternal happiness in the next. What forms human society may take, outside the family unit which has been directly established by God, depend on the free choice of men. But whenever men have established their form of society, the authority of the legitimate rulers thereof is derived indirectly from God and their just laws and commands are binding in conscience on the members of that society. The State may not, therefore, consider itself superior to God, nor may it deny the honor and respect due to God.

Some corporate recognition of God as our Supreme Ruler on the part of the State or any community seems proper and fitting. This obligation does not depend upon any theories of separation or union of Church and State. It does not involve what is sometimes called "sectarian religion." In our own country, where separation of Church and State is the law of the land, this obligation is very adequately cared for. Our Constitution bears witness to a belief in God and His providence; our coinage carries the legend "In God We Trust";

Congress sessions are opened with prayer; there is a national observance of "Thanksgiving Day" and other days of national supplication to God by presidential proclamation, to mention some of the more obvious gestures of recognizing a Divine Providence over the affairs of men.

Without religion man as an individual is subject to injustice and unhappiness because, paradoxical as it may seem, the recognition of man's dependence on God emphasizes man's dignity as a child of God. Without religion the society in which man lives is subject to disorder, disaster and ruin, because without orientation to God as the final source of authority, the ruler of the State tends to invert the true order of things and make man the creature of the State, rather than the State the servant of man. Where religion has been neglected by members of a state, history proves that social, political, and economic decay have always followed. In a very true sense, religion is as necessary for the State as for the individual.

Man naturally religious. As a reasoning creature, man is by nature religious and cannot long refrain from being religious. No matter how strong and ruthless the effort be to stamp out all religion, the spark remains ready to burst into flame as soon as the pressure is removed. No matter how alluring the temptation may be to espouse irreligion, man tends necessarily to revert to religion with all its supposed inconvenience and repressions. Man must have a religion, whether this be the product of his reason alone, or whether it be founded on direct assistance from God, or whether it be a combination of both. Man is by nature religious, and he fulfills this demand of his nature by humbly worshipping God.

The fact that man is by nature religious shows up dramatically whenever man is face to face with catastrophe or any serious emergency which is beyond his power to control. Under such circumstances man tends naturally to turn to God for help, even when he has completely forgotten Him for years. One famous example will suffice to illustrate the point.

During World War II, Captain Eddie Rickenbacker and seven companions were on board a Flying Fortress which was forced to ditch in the South Pacific. For twenty-one days of blistering agony, with only such food and water as God and their ingenuity provided, these men drifted in three tiny rubber life rafts until seven of them were finally rescued. One of the number, copilot Lieutenant James C. Whittaker, published an account of this terrible ordeal. Therein he made this personal statement:

> For me those blazing days represent the greatest adventure a man can have—the one in which he finds his God. . . . I was an agnostic, an atheist, if you will. But from my companions I learned to pray. I saw prayer answered. There are no atheists in the foxholes of Guadalcanal and there can be no atheists in rubber rafts amid whitecaps and sharks. My entire life has been changed by the events that began October 20, 1942. It is a day I'll never forget. (*The Evening Bulletin*, Philadelphia, January 12, 1943.)

It may appear superficially that it is a man's fear and not his inmost promptings or his reasoning that would make him turn to religion at such a time. Actually fear serves chiefly as the trigger to set reason in motion. Once reason is stimulated it will bring man to the practice of religion. Who will say, in the example cited, that the Lieutenant did not have great fear in the face of such grave danger and suffering? And who will deny that his new-found religion was the product of his reason, not of his fear?

REVIEW QUESTIONS

1. How does man's relationship with God differ from that of other earthly creatures?
2. What motivation for worshipping God does reason supply to man?
3. Why is the practice of religion man's duty to God?
4. What is the literal meaning of the word *religion?*
5. What does religion mean in actual practice?

6 Over and above the sense of duty involved, what ought to be true of man's worship of God?

7 Does reason give any clues as to the possibility of reward or punishment in connection with man's duty to worship God?

8 What is the purpose of formal religion?

9 What acts of religion can be deduced from man's threefold relationship with God?

10 What is meant by "subjective" religion?

11 What is meant by "objective" religion?

12 What is the most fundamental reason for the necessity of religion?

13 It is easy enough to understand that both justice and gratitude demand religion, but in what sense can it be claimed that good order demands religion?

14 How is religion necessary for man's happiness?

15 In what sense can it be said that society requires religion?

16 What is meant by the statement: "Man is by nature religious"?

SUGGESTIONS FOR READING

"Religion: Man's Bond With God," *Truths Men Live By,* John A. O'Brien. New York: The Macmillan Company, 1946, pp. 129–211. (Discusses meaning, universality and origin of religion; religious worship, a duty; religion and society; religion and morality; the value of religion. An excellent treatment of foregoing topics, especially the last topic, which points out the practical advantages of religion.)

No Answer Without God, Richard Ginder. The Catholic Information Society, 214 West 31st Street, New York 1, N.Y. 14 pp., 5¢. (Atheism and agnosticism do not make sense. Without God there is no real explanation for anything.)

Religion—Pure and Simple, William J. Quinlan. The Catholic Information Society. 14 pp., 5¢. (The fallacy of religious indifference. Religion is not merely a personal and private affair to be practiced or not as one pleases. God wants us to practice His religion.)

Wide World photo

These *Sunday worshippers* are a familiar scene in any Catholic church. We have a duty to worship God not only privately but also publicly, not only as individuals but also as a community.

Chapter 7

Religion, natural or supernatural

IT IS BOTH REASONABLE and natural for man to wish to worship God, that is, to acknowledge his dependence on God and to render to Him honor, reverence and obedience. This we call *religion,* and we proved in the preceding chapter why it is necessary for man to practice religion. But how is man to know what form this religion is to take?

Natural Religion

Through the exercise of his reason man can arrive at a conviction that God exists and can have a knowledge of many of God's attributes. Man knows through reason that he has a spiritual and immortal soul which is destined for perfect happiness. Likewise, his reason tells him that there is a relationship of dependence on God which requires recognition through the practice of religion. Logically it might be expected that man, through his ability to reason, could fashion for himself a religion that would have all the essentials, be pleasing to God, and meet man's fundamental needs. This would be *natural* religion, based solely on man's reason without any revelation, directly or indirectly, from God. However, there is weighty evidence that seems to indicate that a satisfactory natural religion has never been attained by man. Before drawing any conclusions let us consider what should be the content of a satisfactory natural religion.

The minimum content. It would seem that a satisfactory natural religion should have at least the following qualifications which we will state and analyze briefly:

1. *It should give man sufficient information about the nature of God so as to enable him to worship God intelligently and be safeguarded from serious errors.* From the arguments which we have already deduced to prove the existence of God it would seem that a natural religion could fulfill this requirement satisfactorily. However, history testifies that many races and peoples, when dependent solely on reason for their knowledge of God, have gone astray into the most absurd errors. We know, for example, of the "Sun God" of the Incas of Peru, the various pagan deities of the Greeks and Romans, and so on.

2. *It should give man information as to his origin, nature and true destiny.* Reason has already given us satisfactory information about man's origin and nature. However, beyond indicating the likelihood of reward or punishment, depending on how man fulfills his duty of giving glory to God, and the promise of perfect and permanent happiness for the just in a future life, reason sheds little additional light on man's true destiny. Again history verifies that whole peoples have strayed from what seem to be the sound dictates of reason.

3. *It should give man a fairly definite idea as to how God is to be worshipped and the code of conduct to be followed in order to achieve his destiny.* The natural law, which includes nine of the Ten Commandments, supposedly can be known by reason, but history testifies how far astray man can go when not directed by the revealed word of God. Beyond these dictates of the natural law reason gives man little information as to how he should worship God. We have reasoned out that we owe honor, reverence, love and service to God but even here we may be influenced unconsciously by revelation.

4. *It should do all this with such clarity and certainty that any properly disposed person could find the answers to his religious problems and enjoy reasonable peace of mind.* It is in this regard particularly that natural religion is most deficient. In the first place only one who has much better than average intelligence and the time and opportunity for careful thought can inform himself as to what reason has to offer in the way of religion.

The average person could hardly find the answers to his religious problems. History bears evidence that some of the outstanding pagan thinkers of the past, such as Socrates and Plato and Cicero, have given expression to certain religious truths with startling clarity, but these same men have been grossly in error on other matters of religion or morality which should be just as evident from reason. When these thinkers do happen to strike on a real truth of religion we can never be sure whether this is a product of pure reason or whether it has resulted from their possible contact with revealed truth as found in Judaism or Christianity.

Natural religion insufficient. Through the use of reason man can know that he, a creature composed of body and soul, has a duty to acknowledge dependence on God, his Creator, and to worship Him. We might expect that if man's reason points out the duty of serving and worshipping God, his reason would also be able to indicate clearly the form that this service and worship should take. But man's reason seems to fail him at this point. For history proves as a matter of fact that man has never been able to formulate for himself a satisfactory natural religion. This is not because man has failed to make the effort; there has never been a people on earth, even among the most savage and uncivilized tribes, which has not believed in a Supreme Being and practiced a religion of some kind. But whenever man has had to depend on his own reason to fashion his religion he has always fallen into error. Even in most cultured nations, the great minds who were not directly influenced by revelation made flagrant errors in religion. History proves time and time again that without God's direct help in revealing Himself man has gone astray into the most absurd and even revolting errors. We are forced to conclude that, practically speaking, it is not possible for man to fashion for himself a satisfactory natural religion, based on reason alone.

From the standpoint of reason alone there is something mystifying in the discovery that apart from the special assistance of God man has never succeeded in developing a religion free from serious limitations and even gross errors. Something must have happened to man very early in his history which weakened his intellect and made it difficult for him to think clearly about God. It is especially puzzling to reason to know that God made man for the one purpose of serving and glorifying Him and, seemingly, did not make it possible for man to fulfill this purpose. Reason has no explanation for this mystery, although revelation may have it. Consequently we must conclude that man needs a "supernatural" religion to compensate for this weakness and therefore, at some time and in some way, it was fitting that God reveal Himself to man.

Supernatural Religion

Compensating for man's inadequacy. God created man to love, serve and glorify Him. If man is to fulfill this purpose there must be some way of compensating for his inability to develop adequate religious ideas by himself. We conclude, therefore, that it is appropriate that God help man by revealing to him His truths. This means that in place of a purely natural religion man must have a religion that is supernatural, at least in the manner in which it is made known.

If out of His infinite goodness God destined man to a supernatural end, to a participation in the truths of God which altogether exceed man's human ability to reason for himself, then certainly revelation from God is absolutely necessary. In order to establish this supposition we must be able to show that divine revelation is possible and that it does in fact exist.

Divine revelation possible. There is really no difficulty in proving the possibility of God communicating with man. Since God gave man the power of communicating or revealing his thoughts to his fellow man, it is only reasonable to believe that God Himself could exercise the same power He gave to his creatures. Only the atheist or the agnostic could be unreasonable enough to deny this power to God. Reason tells us that divine revelation is certainly possible.

Divine revelation a fact. Since God created man with an obligation to love and serve Him it would seem to be in accordance with the infinite wisdom, mercy and goodness of God that He reveal Himself in some way to man, especially since it is evident that, left to himself, man is prone to flounder around in error and ignorance. Since divine revelation is both possible and fitting, we are justified in thinking that God has revealed His truths to man. As a matter of fact, we have many claimants who say they possess divine revelation. Practically all of the many religions in the world claim to be based on some kind of divine revelation. All Christian denominations claim to follow a revelation made by God through Jesus Christ. The Jews follow a revelation made by God through Moses and the prophets. Joseph Smith, founder of the Mormons, claimed that he had received a revelation written on golden plates and brought to him by an angel. Mary Baker Eddy, founder of the Christian Scientists, claimed that she had a revelation from

God in founding her religion. Many others who claim to be the bearers of divine revelation could be listed. There is no dearth of claimants.

Identifying Genuine Revelation

Perhaps the number and variety of those claiming to be messengers of divine revelation is worthy of note. But the most noteworthy thing about the various "revelations" is the lack of any semblance of agreement. In fact these rival revelations frequently contradict each other. Thus, one religion says that divorce is forbidden by divine law and another denies this; one Christian religion says that Christ established seven sacraments and another says there are only two sacraments; one religion says that Christ is really and truly present in the Blessed Sacrament and another religion says that He is not present. It is evident that all of these opposed opinions cannot be right. One or the other must be in error on an important point. We must determine which of the conflicting "revelations" is true. The problem, then, is how to distinguish true revelation from false revelation. Here is where our reason must be put to work.

The test of genuine revelation. It is reasonable to assume that, if God does make a revelation for man's guidance, He will make it possible for him to identify it as a true revelation. God's revelation to mankind would be of no benefit if man had no means of determining whether or not it was a true revelation. Reason tells us that genuine revelation from God must have marks by which it can be identified.

If God so willed He could have made known His revelation directly to men by appearing in some visible form accompanied by such demonstration of His omnipotence that everyone would know that it was indeed God who was speaking. Instead, God chose to communicate through selected human persons. Thus it is that every true or supposedly true revelation from God comes to us through the medium of some human messenger. In a way this simplifies our problem of distinguishing true revelation from false revelation, because it makes it possible to investigate the life and character of the supposed bearer of revelation as well as his message. Thus the individual claimants to revelation, whether Jesus Christ, Moses, Joseph Smith, Mary Baker Eddy, or any other, are either God's chosen messengers or they are not. Before an attempt is made to study the supposed revelation, it is possible to examine the life of the individual who claims to have the message from God. If his life and character do not measure up to what one should expect in God's chosen messenger, there is no need to go further. If his life and character are in accord with his claims, then a consideration of his message is in order. The life, character, and message of one who claims to be the bearer of divine revelation must have the unquestionable stamp of God's approval before we can accept the revelation as genuine.

But how shall we proceed with the examination of such claims? Let us select first the claimant whom we wish to investigate and then let us go to the best available records for information as to the life and character of the historical person through whom God is supposed to have made His revelation. If the revelation is genuine it should be reflected in the life and character of the messenger. In addition, the messenger should be able to produce "airtight" credentials to show that God substantiates his claims.

Furthermore, if any particular religious body wishes to establish the fact that God did reveal truths through a certain messenger—truths which are now in the keeping of this organization—let the evidence be brought forth to substantiate that claim. Ideally, such evidence should be in the form of a historical document which proves the claim beyond doubt. Such a document would have to undergo, of course, a rigid scrutiny into its genuineness before being accepted as evidence.

The Christian claim to revelation. Now, Christianity claims that God did make a great and unchangeable revelation through its founder, Jesus Christ. Likewise, it claims that the revelation is still in existence and that it is being taught by the Church as the one, true, final, revelation from God. Furthermore, Christianity avers that it possesses historical documents to prove and support the claim. In this respect it offers the Four Gospels as documentary evidence, that Jesus Christ was God's true envoy, that He made known God's revelation, and that He established His Church to guard and propagate that revelation. It asks that Christ's claim be carefully examined.

Jesus Christ an outstanding claimant. Without doubt Jesus Christ is the most prominent of all those who claim to be bearers of divine revelation. No apology need be made for considering His claim first. He is without question the one who has made the greatest and most lasting impact on the world. His life was most outstanding for its holiness, wisdom, and goodness. If we find that Christ's claims are true then our search for the true revelation is ended. If we find that Christ's claims are not true, we must begin again to search. Although Christ's claims are most extraordinary and His teachings in many cases revolutionary and difficult to accept, millions of the wisest men of all ages have accepted His claims and followed Him. His advent marked the turning point of history so that today we count our years either as B.C. (Before Christ) or A.D. (Anno Domini—the year of our Lord).

Historical sources. What are the sources for our information about Jesus Christ? Fortunately, the original records in which the words and deeds of Jesus Christ were narrated by men of His own day are available to us in documents known as the "Four Gospels." We must examine these Gospels objectively, using the same methods of research and critical analysis that would be used on any important historical document to make sure that it is completely genuine and reliable. Our approach to this investigation is that of the careful historian, using the methods of historical research. In the earlier chapters we employed the principles and methods of a philosopher. Now we must think as a historian.

Once we have satisfied ourselves as to the dependable historical character of the Four Gospels, we can use these sources for information about Jesus Christ, His life, His claims, and the proofs He offered for the truth of these claims. We must first establish that the Four Gospels are reliable historical documents. This we will consider in the following chapter.

REVIEW QUESTIONS

1. What is *natural* religion?
2. What should be the minimum content for a satisfactory natural religion?
3. How difficult would it be for the average person to discover what reason can reveal about religion?
4. Is it not logical to expect that man's reason, which informs him of the existence of a Supreme Being and of his duty to worship, would also prompt him rightly about a satisfactory form of religion?
5. On what basis is natural religion declared to be insufficient for man?
6. How is one to explain the logical inconsistency of the fact that man's reason is unable to find a satisfactory religion?
7. What conclusion does one draw from the inadequacy of man to fashion for himself a satisfactory natural religion?
8. What is a *supernatural* religion?
9. Whence comes divine revelation?
10. Is there any evidence of divine revelation under the Christian dispensation?
11. How can one be sure that a supposed revelation is really from God?
12. What is the Christian claim to revelation?
13. Among all those who claim to be bearers of divine revelation, why is Jesus Christ worthy of first consideration?
14. Where do we get our information about Jesus Christ?
15. How can we be sure that these Gospels are reliable historical documents?

SUGGESTIONS FOR READING

"Revelation: Its Nature and Purpose," *Truths Men Live By*, John A. O'Brien. New York: The Macmillan Company, 1946, Chapter XXVIII, pp. 354–368.

Religion is Reason, Wilfred G. Hurley, C.S.P. The Paulist Press, 401 West 59th Street, New York 19, N.Y., 1934. 18 pp., 10¢. (Discusses the necessity of supernatural religion and revelation.)

Reverend Doctor A. A. Luce, Vice-Chancellor,
by permission of Trinity College, Dublin, Ireland

A page from The Book of Kells, an illuminated manuscript of the *Gospels* in Latin made by Irish monks between the sixth and the ninth centuries A. D. It is generally supposed to belong to the eighth century. This priceless manuscript copy of the Gospels, richly illuminated in color, was used in the divine services at the monastery of Kells in County Meath some forty miles northwest of Dublin. Hence the name, Book of Kells. It is now in the library of Trinity College, Dublin.

Chapter 8

The Gospels, fact or fiction

WE SHALL PRESENT first of all a descriptive account of the Gospels as they are held by the Church. Then we shall consider the tests which the historian employs to establish the dependability of any historical document. Finally we shall apply these tests to the Four Gospels to determine whether or not these documents are dependable sources of information about the life, teachings and claims of Jesus Christ.

Nature of the Gospels

After the fall of Adam, God promised to mankind a Redeemer who would atone for Adam's sin and win back for man the possibility of salvation in heaven. This was a central doctrine of the Jewish religion and for thousands of years the Jews had looked forward with great expectation to the coming of this Redeemer, or Messias. Nevertheless, when Jesus Christ, who claimed that He was the Messias, did appear, the majority of the Jewish people refused to accept Him and their leaders finally brought about His death at the hands of the Romans. The Gospels are the documents which narrate the story of Jesus Christ.

The Christian view. Christ did gather about Him a minority of the Jews—a loyal band of apostles and disciples who believed firmly that He was not only the promised Messias but also the true Son of God. Shortly after Christ's death and ascension into heaven, His apostles announced to the world that the long-expected Messias had come. Through His death on the cross the world was redeemed from sin, and happiness was possible again for every man. This was the "good news" or "good tidings" which the apostles and disciples preached by word of mouth to all whom they could reach. (The English word *Gospel* comes to us as a contraction of two words from the Anglo-Saxon language, meaning "good news" or "good tidings.") These men were fulfilling the command of Christ: "*Preach the gospel to every creature*" *(Mark 16:15).*

The writers of the Gospels. Later, four of these apostles and disciples wrote down separate accounts of these "good tidings." Each account is designated as the Gospel *according to,* for example, *St. Matthew,* to indicate that there are four separate accounts of the same "good tidings." The writers are called *evangelists* from the Latin word which means "good news" or "good tidings."

Two of the evangelists were apostles and two were disciples of other apostles. St. Matthew, an apostle, wrote the First Gospel in the Hebrew Aramaic dialect for the Jews. St. Mark, who was a disciple and companion of the apostle Peter, wrote the Second Gospel in the Greek language for the Gentiles. St.

Luke, a disciple and companion of the apostle Paul, wrote the Third Gospel, also in Greek, for the Gentiles. These three versions of the Gospel of Christ which were written at different times before the destruction of Jerusalem, A.D. 70, are known as the *Synoptic Gospels.* They are so called because they have a common point of view, are strikingly similar to one another, and include substantially the same material, even though one Gospel may mention incidents omitted in another. The Fourth Gospel, composed by the apostle St. John some time before A.D. 97, has been written from a viewpoint quite different from the other three. The Gospel according to St. John has been considered a supplement to the Synoptic Gospels because it contains subject matter and recounts incidents not mentioned in them. All the writers of the Gospels are in complete agreement with one another in regard to the main points of Christ's life, particularly His divinity.

How we propose to use the Gospels. We propose to use the Four Gospels as a source of information about the life, teachings and claims of Jesus Christ, once we have established their dependability as historical documents. But before we attempt to establish the historical value of the Gospels as a preliminary to an examination of the life, teachings and claims of Jesus Christ, we must determine just what it is that we wish to prove. We must also agree upon the meaning of the terms we shall have occasion to use.

For this reason it seems advisable to examine briefly the technique that the historian would use to establish the genuineness of any historical document. Then we will use this same technique to prove that the Four Gospels readily meet the most rigorous tests of genuineness an exacting research historian could demand.

Nature of a Historical Document

A historical document is one that can be used to prove a historical fact. Usually it is an original or official paper (or an authenticated copy), such as the Declaration of Independence, the Constitution of the United States, or the Charter of the United Nations, which can be used to prove that certain actions were taken, or that certain events took place.

Thus, for example, the Constitution of the United States is the official document in which the founding fathers of our country set forth their philosophy of government and established the methods and procedures by which the new nation was to govern itself. In subsequent years, whenever there has been any question as to the rights of the people, or if disputes have arisen as to the form of government intended by the founding fathers, this document has been produced to be studied and to supply the evidence on which correct answers could be based. Of course, no document offered in support of a claim should be accepted until it can be proven genuine and dependable. In order to be considered genuine, a document should have these characteristics: it must be authentic, it must be entire, and it must be trustworthy.

Authentic. This term, when applied to a document, means that it is not a "phony" or a "fake." It's the real thing! The given document was actually written at the time it is supposed to have been written and by the person or persons who are credited with having written it. We could not have any confidence in the Declaration of Independence if we were to find out that it was a forgery made several years after the Revolution had been fought and won, and that those whose names were signed to it never saw or heard of it. If a document is to be considered authentic, we must prove this from evidence in the document itself as well as by evidence entirely separate from the document. In other words, there are both internal and external marks of the authenticity of a document to be searched out. For example, the original copy of the Declaration of Independence on display in the Library of Congress could be proved to be a genuine document in this fashion: search through records, books, papers, periodicals, correspondence, speeches, etc., contemporary with the time when the Declaration was supposed to have been adopted by the Continental Congress in Philadelphia, for any mention of the Declaration and for quotations. This would be the search for *external evidence.* Then one would have experts carefully examine the document itself, the paper or parchment that was used, the ink, the style of writing, the spelling, etc., to see if there is any discrepancy in any of these items when compared with what was known to be in use in 1776. If, for example, one of the complaints alleged against the British king was that he levied an excessive tax on telephones and automobiles, we would know that the document was not genuine because there were no telephones or automobiles when the Declaration of Independence was adopted. Then one would let a handwriting expert compare the signatures to be found on the Declaration with the signatures of these same signers as found in private collections of their letters, etc. This would be the search for *internal evidence* to testify to the genuineness of the document.

Entire. A document is considered to be *entire* when it has not been changed substantially. For example, your copy of the Declaration of Independence could be proven to be "entire" in this fashion: make a representative collection of various printings of the Declaration extending from 1776 to the present. Assemble also a collection of quotations from the Declaration found in the writings and speeches of prominent people, particularly during the period from 1776 to the beginning of the nineteenth century. Examine all this material carefully to see if there is evidence that anything substantial has been added to or subtracted from your copy of the Declaration. If there is no evidence of any substantial change, your copy of the Declaration can be said to be "entire." If a document has been so tampered with by the addition or subtraction of words, sentences, or phrases that the original meaning has been changed or obscured, it is no longer entire, and cannot be considered dependable.

Trustworthy. A document is *trustworthy* if the author is considered qualified to make the statements which bear his name. This means that the author must possess a truthful character, that he is not likely to have been deceived in what he says, and furthermore, that he is in a position to know that what he says is true. We can hardly be blamed for not accepting the testimony of one who does not have a reputation for truthfulness, or who has either made mistakes in judgment or deliberately lied about the facts he relates.

In the instance of the Declaration of Independence there can be no question as to the trustworthiness of the authors. They were known and respected by their fellow men. They were responsible and prominent men in the colonies, and, as they wrote in their document, they literally staked their "lives," their "fortunes," and their "sacred honor" on the successful outcome of the movement which they sponsored. The Declaration of Independence has all the earmarks of a trustworthy document.

In brief, every historical document, if it is to be considered true and dependable, must have these three qualifications: authenticity, integrity, and trustworthiness. If it has these qualifications no one can refuse to accept it as a true and dependable document.

We are now ready to apply these tests to the Four Gospels to see if they meet the requirements for true and dependable historical documents. We shall consider each test separately.

The Gospels Authentic

The Gospels will be established as authentic if we can prove that they were actually written by SS. Matthew, Mark, Luke and John, and that these men were contemporaries of Jesus Christ. For *external evidence* we shall have to depend on the testimony of men other than the writers—men who lived around the time the Gospels were supposedly written. For *internal evidence* we shall look to the Gospels themselves for references to the laws, customs and conditions of the times in which the documents were supposedly written, in order that their accuracy may be checked against other documents of the time. (Please note that this technique is identical with that suggested on page 93 for proving the genuineness of the Declaration of Independence.)

External evidence. External evidence for the authenticity of the Gospels is abundant. From the early days of Christianity, writers, whether friends or enemies of the newly founded Church, accepted without question the genuineness of the Gospels.

The Christian writers[1] of those early days quoted freely from the Gospels and some gave direct testimony to their authenticity. Among these early Christian writers were men of great learning whose writings are available at the present. Some were immediate disciples of the evangelists. Nowhere among these writers can there be found any question of doubt as to the genuine character of the Gospels. Yet these are the men who, knowing at first hand the Gospels and some even the writers of the Gospels, could readily have detected any errors, exaggerations or untruths. Many of these same men laid down their lives as martyrs for the truths of the Gospels. We can hardly ignore their testimony that the Gospels are genuine.

The fact that the Gospels were held in veneration and were in *practical use* all over the Church, within one hundred years of the death of the apostles, while their memory was still vivid, is a conclusive proof of their genuineness.

External evidence for the genuineness of the Gospels is to be found also in the writings of learned pagans and heretics in

[1] Numerous texts from the evangelists are quoted in the letters of Pope Clement (95 A.D.), St. Ignatius of Antíoch (107 A.D.), St. Polycarp of Smyrna (120 A.D.), and other disciples of the apostles. Papias, of Asia Minor, a disciple or associate of St. John, writing about 130 A.D., refers to the Gospels of St. Matthew and St. Mark. St. Justin, St. Irenaeus, Tatian, Tertullian and others, all writing before the end of the second century, bear testimony to the genuineness of the Gospels.

the early centuries of the Church. These men frequently attacked particular doctrines contained in the Gospels but never at any time did they deny the authentic character of the Gospels themselves. This preoccupation with the contents of the Gospels is sufficient proof that the Gospels themselves were genuine and authentic. It would have been much easier for these bitter enemies of Christ and His teachings to denounce the Gospels as forgeries rather than to attack doctrines found therein. It would have been more effective to destroy Christianity by attacking its foundations if there were any weakness therein.

Internal evidence. A critical examination of the text of the Gospels themselves is another way in which to confirm or deny their genuineness. An alert scholar could readily detect anything inaccurate or fictitious about the Gospels by comparing the laws, customs, language, and so forth, of the people described in the Gospels with what was known from other sources to prevail at that time. (The technique for judging such internal evidence is delineated on page 93 in connection with the Declaration of Independence.)

When this technique of criticism is applied to the Gospels no such discrepancies can be found. The writers of the Gospels evidence complete familiarity with the language, customs, habits, laws and manners of the people whom they describe. Modern scholarship has failed to detect any error on the part of the evangelists in their countless references to topography and to the political, social and religious conditions of Palestine during the life of Christ. Those conditions were peculiarly complicated at the time of Christ and then changed suddenly and completely with the advent of war and the complete destruction of Jerusalem and the Temple in A.D. 70. For these reasons both ancient and modern historians—even those who are enemies of Christianity—agree that the Gospels must have been written at the time and by the writers to whom they are ascribed.

Both external and internal evidence compel us to believe that the Gospels are genuine or authentic, that is, they were written by SS. Matthew, Mark, Luke and John before the close of the first century of Christianity. No successful attempt has ever been made to disprove this.

The Gospels Trustworthy

The proof that the Gospels are genuine or authentic, that is, that they were written by the men whose names they bear, is a considerable step forward in establishing the historical dependability of the Gospels. The next logical step is to prove that these same writers were, themselves, completely trustworthy. Bluntly put, this means that we must satisfy ourselves that the writers did not intend or wish to deceive others and also that there is no possibility that they were themselves deceived.

The writers' knowledge of what they wrote. The evangelists knew, intimately, the facts of which they wrote. St. Matthew and St. John had been companions of Christ and were eyewitnesses to the events about which they wrote. St. Mark wrote his Gospel under the guidance of St. Peter, for whom he served as a helper and companion; St. Luke, under the guidance of St. Paul. Both of these evangelists lived in constant association and communion with Christ's contemporaries.

The writers not deceivers. The story of the life of each of the evangelists is sufficient guarantee of his sincerity and honesty. Besides, what had they to gain by deception? From a worldly standpoint they had nothing to gain and everything to lose by testifying to the life and teachings of Christ. All except St. John died as martyrs for the truth of what they wrote. It is not reasonable to think that they would die willingly as martyrs in defending what they knew to be untrue. But even had the writers of the Gospels wished to deceive, they could not, in the circumstances under which they wrote, be untruthful. They wrote for contemporaries of the events they narrated or for men who had known those contemporaries. Many of the incidents about which they wrote had been witnessed by thousands of others. Moreover, these same accounts were preached or read publicly to those who had witnessed them. They could not, without detection, have published a false account.

Finally, the evangelists, who came from humble walks of life, could hardly have invented the commanding personality and the deep but flawless character of Christ. The Christ who emerges from the Gospels could flay the Scribes and Pharisees with biting words as "hypocrites" and "brood of vipers" for laying heavier burdens on the people than they could bear (Matthew 23:13–16); He could scourge the money-changers out of the temple (John 2:13–16); but He could also say: *"Come to me all you that labor and are burdened and I will give you rest. Take my yoke upon you and learn from me, for I am meek and humble of heart" (Matthew 11:28–29);* or *"Let the little children come to me, and do not hinder them, for of such is the kingdom of God" (Mark 10:14)*. Even His enemies had to pay tribute to the Man who could hold the crowd enthralled with His teaching: *"Never did any man speak as does this man!" (John 7:40–47).* Then there was the triumphal entry into Jerusalem with hosannas to the Son of David and the cry: *"Blessed is he who comes in the name of the Lord!" (Matthew 21:9),* and a few days later, the tragic death on Calvary, nailed to the cross between two thieves. The Christ who stands forth so nobly, so lovably, so flawlessly in the Gospels; whose character has stood the test of minute scrutiny throughout the centuries, could not have been invented by one even greater than Shakespeare. There is much less likelihood that the four humble Jewish disciples of Christ could invent his outstanding and unique personality, especially since they, like all the members of their race, were expecting a Messias who would restore the kingdom of David, a temporal kingdom, and not the spiritual kingdom preached by Christ.

The writers not deceived. If the evangelists in good faith were themselves deceived, they were not alone. For the teachings and works of Christ which they reported were, in many instances, witnessed by thousands. Certainly all those who witnessed His many miracles or who personally experienced the benefit of these miracles, believed, as well as all the apostles and disciples of Christ, what they saw with their own eyes. Even Christ's enemies testified that *"no man ever performed the works of this man."* Some of His enemies, it is true, tried to discount His marvelous works by attributing them to the power of Satan, but they did not *deny* these works. It is hardly reasonable to suppose that everybody who witnessed Christ's works was deceived. Yet this must be conceded if it is granted that the evangelists were deceived.

The Gospels Entire

Having proved that the Gospels are genuine or authentic, that is, that they were really written by the men whose names they bear, and that these men were truthful and honest and not likely to have been themselves deceived by the events they narrate, we have almost completed our task of establishing the historical dependability of the Gospels. The final step is to prove that the Gospels as we have them today are substantially *intact,* that is, that they have not been changed or altered since the evangelists wrote them. If changes have been made to such an extent that the Gospels no longer retain their original meaning, then we can hardly consider them dependable historical documents.

No changes after wide diffusion. At present it would be utterly impossible to make any substantial changes in the Gospels because of the wide diffusion of the Gospels among Christian peoples throughout the world. Copies of the Gospels are in the hands of Catholics everywhere from the pope down to the humblest layman. In addition, copies of the Gospels are available to Protestants, Jews and unbelievers. Under these conditions it would be impossible today to make any substantial changes in these documents without detection and denouncement. But this situation has prevailed almost from the earliest years of the Church. The Gospels have appeared in every known language. Scriptural scholars have been able to trace back some translations of the Gospels to the first quarter of the second century. As a consequence there has been wide diffusion of the Gospels almost from the very beginning with copies available to both friends and enemies of the Church. When you couple this with the fact that the Gospels were held in the highest esteem, it would have been absolutely impossible for substantial alterations to have been made.

No changes before translations. Could not, however, alterations have been made before the Gospels were translated and widely scattered? The answer is: by no means! For during this period the apostles or their immediate disciples were still living. The apostles and disciples of Christ not only preached the Gospels continuously but they defended them with their lives. It is inconceivable that they would have tolerated any changes. In fact, the apostle St. Paul, when writing to the Galatians, bids them to beware of false gospels: *If anyone preach a gospel to you other than that which you have received, let him be anathema (Galatians 1:9).*

There is also every reason to believe that the early Christians would not have permitted any changes to be made in the Gospels. These Gospels were read publicly in the churches at that time and the early Christians knew them well; they loved and respected them so much that many of these Christians suffered martyrdom for their belief in them.

A much stronger proof that the Gospels were preserved substantially unchanged during this pre-translation period can be found in the writings of the early fathers and doctors of the Church,[2] who quoted profusely from the Gospels. In fact,

[2] The fathers and doctors of the Church were learned men in the early Church who explained and commented upon the doctrines contained in the Gospels.

their quotations are so numerous that it has been said that the Four Gospels could be reconstructed almost entirely from the quotations found in their writings. Now it is of particular interest to note that these gospel quotations used by the fathers of the Church are substantially the same as the passages which we read in the Gospels today, indicating, surely, that there have been no substantial changes from the original Gospels.

Agreement of all old manuscripts. Actually there are about 13,000 old manuscripts of the Bible in existence, a substantial portion of which contain the Four Gospels. These manuscript copies from all countries have been diligently scrutinized by a multitude of learned scholars, who have done painstaking research through the records and monuments of the past. Many of these investigations have been made by scholars who were not favorable to Christianity. The results of all this research have proven conclusively that all duly authenticated manuscripts, even the most ancient, agree substantially with each other. They agree also with innumerable quotations contained in the writings of the fathers and doctors of the Church. Only one conclusion is possible. The Gospels have come down to us today substantially unchanged from the way they were written in the beginning. The Gospels have, therefore, the integrity which is required for a dependable historical document. (See page 93 for the technique suggested for establishing the integrity of present-day copies of the Declaration of Independence.)

The Gospels Reliable Historical Documents

We now have complete assurance that we can rely upon the Four Gospels as dependable historical documents. They have stood the tests and have proved to be genuine, trustworthy, and entire. From here on we are at liberty to use the Gospels freely for whatever they can tell us concerning their central figure, Christ.

Christianity offers these Four Gospels as historical documentary evidence that its teachings are based upon truths revealed by God through His ambassador, Jesus Christ. We shall use these Gospels as a source of information about the life, character and teachings of Jesus Christ.

REVIEW QUESTIONS

1 What are the Gospels?
2 What are the derivations for the words *Gospel* and *evangelist?*
3 What is the significance of the word *Gospel?*
4 In what way do we wish to use the Gospels?
5 Who were the writers of the Gospels?
6 For whom were the Gospels written?
7 What is meant by the *Synoptic Gospels?*
8 What is a historical document?
9 How can we establish that a certain document is a reliable historical document?
10 What is meant by saying that a document is authentic or genuine?
11 Specifically, how can the authentic character of a document be established?
12 How can the integrity or substantial intactness of a document be established?
13 How can the trustworthy character of a document be established?
14 Give one example of *external* evidence to show that the Gospels are authentic.
15 Give one example of *internal* evidence to show that the Gospels are authentic.
16 Give one example of the type of evidence used to show that the Gospels are trustworthy.
17 Give one example of the type of evidence used to show that the Gospels are substantially intact, or have the quality of integrity.

SUGGESTIONS FOR READING

"The Historical Character of the Gospels," *Truths Men Live By,* John A. O'Brien. New York: The Macmillan Company, 1946, Chapter XXIX, pp. 368–398.

What is the Bible? John Corbett, S.J. The Paulist Press, 401 West 59th Street, New York 19, N.Y., 1927. 32 pp., 10¢. (Names the books in the Bible, explains *inspiration,* and tells how we know that the Bible is inspired.)

It's the Gospel Truth, Richard Ginder. Catholic Information Society, 214 West 31st Street, New York 1, N.Y. 14 pp., 5¢. (The Gospels have come down to us unchanged; they are trustworthy.)

We Swear By It, Richard Ginder. Catholic Information Society. 15 pp., 5¢. (Gospels are authentic history.)

Where We Got the Bible, Henry G. Graham. St. Louis: B. Herder Book Company, 1924. 166 pp. (A popularly written book telling how the Bible came to be and how it has been preserved intact down to the present day. Refutes various false charges made against the Church because of its alleged attitude toward the Bible and Bible reading in general.)

The Catholic Church and the Bible. Wilfred G. Hurley, C.S.P. The Paulist Press, 1934. 24 pp., 10¢.

United Press photo

On trial for His life. An "Ecce Homo" by the great Italian painter, Titian, now in the National Gallery of Dublin, Ireland.

Chapter 9

Christ's claims

Christ in the Gospels

HAVING ESTABLISHED the Gospels as dependable historical documents, we may now use them freely to obtain information about Jesus Christ, His life, His claims, and His teachings. In every Gospel it is clearly evident that Christ is the central figure, the commanding personality, whose every word and action is kept constantly before us. In fact, the Gospels were written solely to tell us what Jesus said and what He did. In concluding his Gospel, St. John tells us: *There are, however, many other things that Jesus did; but if every one of these should be written, not even the world itself, I think, could hold the books that would have to be written" (John 21:25).* Never for a moment is there reason to doubt that Jesus Christ actually lived and walked this earth. For no man in history is there more varied and convincing evidence that he actually existed.

The testimony of contemporary writers, both Jewish and pagan, confirms that Christ lived at the time indicated by the evangelists. The Jewish historian, Flavius Josephus (A.D. 37–98), says: "There lived about this time Jesus, a wise man, if it be right to call him a man, for he was a doer of wonderful deeds." The Roman historian, Tacitus (A.D. 55–120 approx.), records that "Christ was put to death by the Procurator, Pontius Pilate, in the reign of Tiberius" (*Annals* xv, 44). Even without the testimony of these contemporary writers, the very tangible impact of Christ's life and teachings on the world, the fact of the marvelous spread of Christianity in the face of the most ruthless persecution, together with the continued existence of the Church down through the centuries are proof enough of the real existence of Christ.

We intend to use the Gospels to establish certain definite truths about Christ. Thus we want to make sure that He was truly man, that He claimed to be the Messias, and more, that He claimed to be the Son of God. Once we have established these claims then we shall search the Gospels for proofs that the claims are true.

It was not thought necessary to quote in full every reference to the Gospels. It is much better to read the citation in its own context. Therefore, it must be emphasized that the words, *we shall search the Gospels for proof,* are to be understood literally by the reader and acted upon. In the space of the next two paragraphs, for example, there are eleven citations from the Gospels: four from St. Matthew, four from St. John, and three from St. Luke. Each citation refers to an incident in the life of Christ, the nature of which is indicated only by a word or a brief phrase. The reader is urged to have his New Testament at hand so that he may read for himself each of the citations in its own context.

Christ true man. As we read through the Gospels we find abundant evidence to show that Jesus Christ was truly man. With a little effort we can piece together facts which make it clear that Christ had a human nature like all of us. Without any claim at completeness, but merely as an illustration, we cite the following human characteristics of Christ which are recounted in the Gospels: Christ was born and laid in His manger-crib because there was no room for Him in the inn (Luke 2:4–7). For some time after birth He remained a helpless infant and had to be carried about in arms like other children (Luke 2:28). He grew up as any other child would do. Meanwhile He was subject to His parents, and *advanced in wisdom and age and grace before God and men (Luke 2: 51–52).*

Christ was subject to the same bodily needs as other men. He suffered from hunger (Matthew 4:2) and thirst (John 19: 28) and fatigue (John 4:6). He was subject to temptation (Matthew 4:1), and was borne down by suffering (Matthew 26:39). He loved His friends (John 11:5) and wept over their misfortunes (John 11:35). Finally, after living like other men, He suffered death like other men, although He died the cruel and unjust death of the cross (Matthew 27:50).

Christ's Claim to Be the Messias

Throughout the Old Testament, in the writings of the Hebrew prophets, there are implicit and explicit references to a belief in a Messias whom God would raise up in the course of time to redeem His people and to win back for them eternal salvation. The whole Jewish religion centered largely about this promised Redeemer whose coming was, in many respects, foretold in minute detail.

Sent by God. The Gospels show in many places that Christ claimed, both privately and publicly, to be the promised Messias sent by God. Thus in conversing with the woman at Jacob's well, in reply to her statement, *"I know that the Messias is coming (who is called Christ), and when he comes he will tell us all things." Jesus said to her, "I who speak with thee am he" (John 4:25–26).* When eating the Last Supper with His apostles, Jesus prayed to His heavenly Father that those to whom He was sent *"may know thee, the only true God, and him whom thou hast sent, Jesus Christ" (John 17:3).*

Many times in public Christ made such claims; for example, on the occasion of His teaching in the synagogue at Nazareth: *He entered the synagogue on the Sabbath and stood up to read. And the volume of Isaias the prophet was handed to him. And after he opened the volume, he found the place where it was written, "The Spirit of the Lord is upon me; because he has anointed me; To bring good news to the poor he has sent me, to proclaim to the captives release, and sight to the blind; To set at liberty the oppressed, to proclaim the acceptable year of the Lord, and the day of recompense." And closing the volume he gave it back to the attendant and sat down. And the eyes of all in the synagogue were gazing on him. But he began to say to them, "Today this scripture has been fulfilled in your hearing" (Luke 4:16–21).*

Taught with authority. Christ claimed to be a divinely appointed legate with supreme authority to teach mankind. *"He who believes in me, believes not in me but in him who sent me. . . . He who rejects me, and does not accept my words, has one to condemn him. . . . For I have not spoken on my own authority, but he who sent me, the Father, has commanded me what I should say, and what I should declare" (John 12: 44–49).*

Moreover, Christ taught with far greater authority and finality than Moses or any of the other prophets. Thus He restored the original law on the indissolubility of marriage which Moses had relaxed (Matthew 19:6–9). He declared

Himself a greater prophet than Jonas (Matthew 12:41). He claimed power to interpret God's own law concerning the Sabbath (Mark 2:28). His instruction to His apostles was all-embracing: *"Go, therefore, and make disciples of all nations, . . . teaching them to observe all that I have commanded you" (Matthew 28:19–20).*

All obliged to accept His teaching. Christ made it clear that everlasting life depends upon man's acceptance of His teaching: *"Amen, amen, I say to you, he who hears my word, and believes him who sent me, has life everlasting" (John 5:24).* Also He said: *"He who believes and is baptized shall be saved, but he who does not believe shall be condemned" (Mark 16: 16).* And, again: *"Now this is everlasting life, that they may know thee, the only true God, and him whom thou hast sent, Jesus Christ" (John 17:3).*

His claim generally known. There can be no question that Christ claimed openly and repeatedly to be the Messias, a divinely appointed legate, with supreme authority to teach mankind. It is clear also that the people in general knew that He made this claim. Nicodemus, a ruler of the Jews, said to Christ on one occasion, *"Rabbi, we know that thou hast come a teacher from God, for no man can work these signs that thou workest unless God be with him" (John 3:2).* The two disciples on the way to Emmaus spoke to the "stranger" in their midst, *"Concerning Jesus of Nazareth, who was a prophet, mighty in work and word before God and all the people" (Luke 24:19).*

Christ's Claim to Be Divine

We have, thus far, established the fact that Christ really *claimed* to be the Messias, a divinely appointed legate. Once this claim has been proven to be valid and true we would be obligated to accept Christ's teachings and pattern our lives accordingly. But Christ is said to have made a still greater claim than to be merely God's legate. He claimed that He was Himself divine, the only-begotten Son of God. Before proceeding further we must make certain that this was actually Christ's claim and that there is no possibility of explaining it away.

Claim frequently mentioned. On searching through the Gospels it is amazing to find how variously and how repeatedly Christ clearly makes this claim to be divine. Sometimes it appears in passages in which He speaks and acts as God; for example, when He forgives sin or raises the dead to life (Mark 2:5, 5:35–43; Luke 7:49, 7:12–15; John 11:38–44). Sometimes it is implicit in His claim to the prerogatives of divinity, as when He said: *"Amen, amen, I say to you, before Abraham came to be, I am" (John 8:58).* On this occasion His hearers fully understood the meaning of these words because they took up stones to cast at Him as a blasphemer.

From the many gospel passages that we could cite in proving both that Christ claimed to be divine and that those about Him understood this claim in a literal sense we shall select four. Two of these passages refer to His enemies who oppose the claim, call it blasphemy, and would put Him to death because of it. Two passages refer to His disciples who accept the claim and, in so doing, make profound acts of faith.

Walking in Solomon's portico. On one occasion Jesus was walking in Solomon's portico in the temple of Jerusalem, when the Jews gathered around Him and asked, *"How long dost thou keep us in suspense? If thou art the Christ, tell us openly." Jesus answered them, "I tell you and you do not believe. The works that I do in the name of my Father, these bear witness concerning me. But you do not believe because you are not of my sheep. My sheep hear my voice, and I know them and they follow me. And I give them everlasting life; and they shall never perish, neither shall anyone snatch them out of my hand. What my Father has given me is greater than all; and no one is able to snatch anything out of the hand of my Father. I and the Father are one." The Jews therefore took up stones to stone him. Jesus answered them, "Many good works have I shown you from my Father. For which of these works do you stone* *me?" The Jews answered him, "Not for a good work do we stone thee, but for blasphemy, and because thou, being a man, makest thyself God" (John 10:24–33).*

On trial for His life. On another occasion Christ affirmed His divinity when He was on trial for His life, standing under oath before the high priest. The false witnesses who had been gathered in to testify against Him had botched their job by making contradictory statements. The high priest, therefore, spoke directly to Jesus and asked, "*Art thou the Christ, the Son of the Blessed One?" And Jesus said to him, "I am. And you shall see the Son of Man sitting at the right hand of the Power and coming with the clouds of heaven." But the high priest tore his garments and said, "What further need have we of witnesses? You have heard the blasphemy. What do you think?" And they all condemned him as liable to death (Mark 14:61–64).*

Now it was because He claimed to be God that Jesus was put to death. When compelled by Pilate to put their cards on the table in demanding the execution of Jesus, the Jewish leaders said: "*We have a Law, and according to that Law he must die, because he has made himself Son of God" (John 19:7).*

Faith of His apostles. In contrast to the actions of Christ's enemies, His apostles accepted Christ's claim to divinity with acts of profound faith. Thus on one occasion Jesus had asked His disciples, "*Who do men say the Son of Man is?*" After they had told Him what other men said, He asked them, "*But who do you say that I am?*" Simon Peter, answering in the name of all said, "*Thou art the Christ, the Son of the living God.*" Far from objecting to this tremendous declaration, Christ approved and confirmed it by saying, "*Blessed art thou, Simon Bar-Jona, for flesh and blood has not revealed this to thee, but my Father in Heaven" (Matthew 16:14–17).*

After Jesus had miraculously fed five thousand, the crowd insisted on following Him, hoping for other miracles. Jesus rebuked them because they sought the food that perishes. It was at this time that Jesus made the startling promise that He would feed them on the bread of eternal life which was His flesh for the life of the world. When His hearers murmured and objected to this, Jesus made His statement all the stronger by saying, "*Amen, amen, I say to you, unless you eat the flesh of the Son of Man, and drink his blood, you shall not have life in you*" *(John 6:54). From this time many of his disciples turned back and no longer went about with him. Jesus therefore said to the Twelve, "Do you also wish to go away?" Simon Peter therefore answered, "Lord, to whom shall we go? Thou hast words of everlasting life, and we have come to believe and to know that thou art the Christ, the Son of God" (John 6:67–70).*

Certainty that the claim was made. In these passages from the Gospels, Christ clearly and positively declares His divinity. Both His friends and His enemies understood this to be His claim and they reacted accordingly. His enemies would put Him to death. His friends would believe and stand by Him. In all, thousands of persons must have heard Him make these claims or have learned about them from others. He claimed to be God, and His hearers understood exactly what He meant. But to make a claim which is properly understood is one thing. It is quite another thing to prove that the claim is true. We have now reached the point at which we must see whether or not Christ gave proof of the truth of His claims.

REVIEW QUESTIONS

1 As historical documents, what purpose do the Gospels serve?

2 Approximately what proportion of the Gospels are devoted to the life and teachings of Jesus Christ?

3 Apart from the Gospels, do we have any certainty that Christ actually lived and walked this earth?

4 Why is it important to prove that Christ was truly man as well as truly God?

5 How can we prove from the Gospels that Christ was truly man?

6 What does *Messias* mean?
7 What does *legate* mean?
8 Give one instance from the Gospels to show that Christ really claimed to be the Messias.
9 Have we any assurance that Christ's claim to be the Messias was generally known among the people?
10 Is there evidence in the Gospels to show that Christ claimed to be God, and not merely an ambassador of God?
11 Is there evidence to show that the apostles really believed in the divinity of Christ before His death and resurrection?
12 If it be established with certainty that Christ claimed to be God, why is further proof demanded in apologetics?

SUGGESTIONS FOR READING

"The Divinity of Christ," *Truths Men Live By,* John A. O'Brien. New York: The Macmillan Company, 1946, Chapter XXVII, pp. 341–354.

"What Think Ye of Christ?" *Rebuilding a Lost Faith,* John L. Stoddard. New York: P. J. Kenedy & Sons, 1924, Chapter VIII, pp. 70–79.

He Was God, Richard Ginder. Catholic Information Society, 214 West 31st Street, New York 1, N.Y. 15 pp., 5¢. (The Gospels say clearly that Jesus Christ was God.)

The Promised Messiah, Richard Ginder. Catholic Information Society. 15 pp., 5¢. (Christ was actually God.)

Is Christ Really God? L. Rumble, M.S.C. Radio Replies Press Society, St. Paul 1, Minnesota. 31 pp., 15¢. (Deals with the historical worth of the Gospels and proof for the divinity of Christ.)

The Prophets and the Messiah, Marshall Schug, O.F.M. Cap. Catholic Information Society. 16 pp., 5¢. (The Messias as promised and foretold in the Old Testament.)

Wide World photo

The Italian sculptor, Lorenzo Ferri, seems to have captured in this *sculptured head of Jesus Christ* some of the nobility of character which stands forth so clearly from the pages of the Gospels.

Chapter 10

Christ proved His claims, I

Importance to Christianity

FROM OUR STUDY OF the Four Gospels, we are now certain that Jesus Christ really claimed to be not only the promised Messias, but more—the Son of God Himself. This is a tremendous claim which, if it is to be sustained, must be backed up with irrefutable evidence. If Christ be not God, then Christianity has no meaning and no reason for existence. Therefore, the proof that Christ is divine is the most important proof in apologetics. Of what value is it to have historical documents which give us the teachings of Christ if He be not God as He claimed?

Now if man is to believe that Christ is the Son of God whose teachings he is obligated to accept, it is only reasonable to expect that God has placed the seal of His approval on Christ in such a way that no reasonable man who examines the evidence can deny His divinity.

The nature of the evidence. Our problem, then, is to prove that Christ gave undeniable evidence to support His claim to divinity. Such evidence should be both internal and external. Internal evidence is that which shines forth from the character of Christ. We can expect this evidence to appear in all phases of His life, especially in the purity, sincerity and sublimity of His life as well as in His knowledge, wisdom, prudence and compassion. External evidence is to be looked for in the credentials offered by Christ Himself or by God in support of the claim. These credentials must be in the form of visible or audible signs or marks of such a nature that only God can bring them to pass. The only credentials that meet this requirement are either miracles which surpass all the powers of nature, or prophecies, the accurate foretelling of future events which only God Himself can know.

The Character of Christ

Character is defined as the sum total of all those qualities which go to make up a person. However, it is chiefly on the basis of what a man says and of what he does that we judge his character to be good or bad. In the case of one who claims to be divine it is only reasonable to expect that the teachings and life of such a one should be in perfect harmony with his claim. In the case of Christ there is ample evidence to support the claim that He was not merely an ordinarily good man, but that He had a superhuman nature, a character sublime.

Viewed as a human person, Christ "was a man of superb courage and stainless character. He was firm but not obstinate. The poor tradesman from Galilee had no fear of the proud and powerful Pharisees. He scourged them in a terrible invective for their hypocrisy, their avarice, and their hardness of heart. He knew that their fury could be sated only by His blood, yet He never ceased to whip them with the lash of righteous indignation.[1] Several times He was on the brink of destruction. Once a raging mob had swept Him to the verge of a cliff, but, at the last moment, He eluded their grasp.[2] In the hour of His Passion, caught in the toils of His enemies, He made no appeal, no apology, no retraction of His doctrine. No cry for mercy escaped Him, when the pitiless scourges lacerated His flesh, nor when His sacred hands and feet were nailed to the Cross. Bitter though His enemies were, they were silent when He challenged them to charge Him with sin.[3] He was the only man that ever lived who could stand up before His enemies and defy them to convict Him of a single fault. The traitor, Judas, confessed, 'I have sinned in betraying innocent blood.'[4] At His trial, when His foes strained every nerve against Him, neither Pilate nor Herod could find any guilt in Him:[5] His character scrutinized in the fierce light of savage hatred showed not a stain. — He was no self-seeker, no respecter of wealth. He fled when the multitude sought to make Him king.[6] He had not enough money to live without alms.[7] He could not pay the temple dues without a miracle.[8] He whose ability might have borne Him to the highest position had not 'whereon to lay His head.'[9] He preferred to be a teacher of truth, to wander about poor and homeless. He was firm, but not obstinate. He refused to abate His teaching to win the companionship of the young ruler.[10] Yet He knew how to bend when no principle was at

[1] Matthew 23, 16:21; John 11:48.
[2] Luke 4:30; cf. Matthew 12:15; John 8:59, 10:39, 11:53.
[3] John 8:46.
[4] Matthew 27:4.
[5] Luke 23:13–15.
[6] John 6:15.
[7] Luke 8:3.
[8] Matthew 17:23–26.
[9] *Ibid.* 8:20.
[10] Mark 10:22.

stake. He sought to escape, even by hiding, the importunities of the Syrophoenician woman who implored Him with piteous cries to heal her daughter, but, at last, touched by her profound humility, He yielded."[11] (Sheehan, *Apologetics and Catholic Doctrine*, pp. 105–106.)

His teachings. In reading through the Gospels to discover Christ's teachings one fact stands out clearly: His teachings are sublime. They far surpass in sublimity and beauty, in wisdom and goodness, the teachings of any other man. It is apparent now in the written record as it was apparent in the time of Christ that *"Never has man spoken as this man" (John 7:46).* The world has never known another philosopher or religious leader whose teachings can compare in wisdom and holiness with the doctrines which Christ taught. This is the testimony of Christ's friends and enemies of the present day just as it was the testimony of those living at the time of Christ, and of those who have lived down through the ages. Even those who deny Christ's divinity testify to the sublimity and goodness of His teachings.

His life. The admitted sublimity and goodness of Christ's teachings make it all the more important that His life also should be sublime. Christ taught others: *"Be ye perfect as your heavenly Father is perfect."* What a reflection on Christ's character it would be to find that He taught one doctrine but practiced another! Fortunately the evidence is overwhelming in showing that Christ lived a perfect life. Page after page of the Gospels record such instances as these: Christ's countless acts of humility, meekness, kindness and generosity; His compassion for the sick and infirm; His mercies of healing for the blind, the deaf, the dumb, the lame, and the lepers; His power over the devils; His forgiveness of sins; His pardoning of enemies, even of His executioners. All these evidences prove beyond a doubt that Christ lived an exemplary life, a life completely in harmony with His teachings and with the nature of

[11] Matthew 15:24; Mark 7:24.

the divinity He claimed. This is the testimony of all who knew Him, even His enemies.

The rationalist writer, Lecky, says:

> It was reserved for Christianity to present to the world an ideal character, which, through all the changes of eighteen centuries, has inspired the hearts of men with an impassioned love; has shown itself capable of acting on all ages, nations, temperaments, and conditions; has been not only the highest pattern of virtue, but the strongest incentive to its practice, and has exercised so deep an influence that it may be truly said that the simple record of three short years of active life has done more to regenerate and soften mankind, than all the disquisitions of philosophers, and all the exhortations of moralists. (*History of European Morals,* Vol. II, p. 8. 3rd ed. Longmans, Green & Co., Inc., 1911.)

Surely we can do no less than to admit that His character was in complete accord with His claim to divinity.

The Miracles of Christ

The fact that Christ's life and teachings are in complete harmony with His claim to be the Son of God is an important step in proving that His claim is true. At the very least it creates a presumption in His favor. Deception of any kind is hardly consistent with teaching a sublime doctrine and leading a blameless life. But we must seek for further evidence, particularly that type of evidence which signifies the approval of God. The working of miracles would be one way in which God could signify His approval of Christ's claim to be divine. We have said that a miracle is a visible happening which surpasses all the powers of nature, and must be attributed directly to the intervention of God. Granting that we do not know everything that nature *can* do, we know, nevertheless, certain things that nature *cannot* do, and we can, therefore, identify real miracles when they occur.

Fortunately for our purposes, the life of Christ is filled with miracles of all kinds which fall readily into three classes: (1) those involving power over inanimate objects, (2) the healing of the sick, and (3) the raising of the dead to life. Since there are so many miracles of such varied types, there is a large margin for error to provide for whatever seeming miracles might later turn out to be caused by hidden forces in nature.

In searching through the Gospels for examples of miracles, one gets the impression that some of these miracles, especially the particularly important miracles, are so surrounded by circumstances and witnesses as to make it impossible in subsequent years to deny them or to explain them away. We shall mention briefly only the most striking miracles under each class.

Miracles and inanimate nature. Many of Christ's miracles were wrought on lifeless matter: He changed water into wine at the marriage feast in Cana (John 2:1–11); He fed five thousand with five loaves and two fishes (Matthew 14: 14-21); He stilled a storm with a word (Matthew 8:23–27); He walked upon the waters of the sea (Mark 6:48–51).

Miracles of healing. On numerous occasions Christ healed the sick, the blind, the lame, the dumb, the epileptic, by a mere word and sometimes from a distance. The Gospels do not mention all of Christ's miracles because on more than one occasion the evangelists simply state that Christ cured of diverse diseases *all* those who were brought to Him. We mention but a few examples. (1) On one occasion Christ cured a leper by a mere word; on another occasion He cured ten lepers although leprosy, even today, is considered incurable, especially in the advanced stages (Matthew 8:2–3; Luke 17: 12–19). (2) Christ also cured a man who was affected with paralysis (Matthew 9:2–8). The servant of the centurion was healed by Christ at a distance without even seeing or speaking to him (Matthew 8:5–13). (3) He cured at least seven blind persons (Matthew 9:27–31, 12:22, 20:30–34; Mark 8:22–26, 10:46–52; Luke 18:35–43; John 9:1–7). (4) He restored hearing and speech to a deaf-mute (Mark 7:32–35).

THE MAN BORN BLIND. Of the miracles cited above, there is the cure of a man born blind described in the ninth chapter of St. John's Gospel. This is particularly valuable for our purpose because Christ specifically referred to it as proof of His divine power. Furthermore the circumstances of the miracle are such as to anticipate practically all the objections that might be brought up against the reality of the miracle. For that reason we will quote from the gospel account the entire incident, making appropriate comments.

And as he was passing by, he saw a man blind from birth. And his disciples asked him, "Rabbi, who has sinned, this man or his parents, that he should be born blind?" Jesus answered, "Neither has this man sinned, nor his parents, but the works of God were to be made manifest in him. I must do the works of him who sent me while it is day; night is coming, when no one can work. As long as I am in the world I am the light of the world." When he had said these things, he spat on the ground and made clay with the spittle, and spread the clay over his eyes, and said to him, "Go, wash in the pool of Siloe" (which is interpreted "sent"). So he went away, and washed, and returned seeing (John 9:1–7).

In the passage just quoted, note that Christ refers to His heavenly Father, who sent Him and whose works He must do. Also note that Christ refers to Himself as the "light of the world." Meanwhile, the restoration of sight to the blind man stirs up some controversy. The neighbors are amazed and strive to explain away the miracle by denying that the "seeing" man now before them is the same as the blind man they knew.

The neighbors therefore and they who were wont to see him before as a beggar, began saying, "Is not this he who used to sit and beg?" Some said, "It is he." But others said, "By no means, he only resembles him." Yet the man declared, "I am he." They therefore said to him, "How were thy eyes opened?" He answered, "The man who is called Jesus made clay and anointed my eyes, and said to me, 'Go to the pool of Siloe and wash.' And I went and washed, and I see." And they said to him, "Where is he?" He said, "I do not know." They took him who had been blind to the Pharisees. Now it was a Sabbath on which Jesus made the clay and opened his eyes. Again, therefore, the Pharisees asked him how he received his sight. But he said to them, "He put clay upon my eyes, and I washed, and I see." Therefore some of the Pharisees said, "This man is not from God, for he does not keep the Sabbath." But others said, "How can a man who is a sinner work these signs?" And there was a division among them. Again therefore they said to the blind man, "What dost thou say of him who opened thy eyes?" But he said, "He is a prophet" (John 9:8–17).

In this second excerpt from the gospel account of the man born blind, it is interesting to note that the Pharisees have raised two points that we have considered in showing that Christ has really proved His claim to be divine. We argued that because Christ's life was blameless there was no conflict there with His claim to divinity. One Pharisee, falsely judging Christ's healing on the Sabbath, used the same argument in reverse to show that *"This man is not from God, for he does not observe the Sabbath."* Another Pharisee did not agree with him because, as he argued correctly, *"How can a man who is a sinner work these signs?"* This is the point we have been making when we say that Christ's miracles prove His claim to be divine.

The Jews therefore did not believe of him that he had been blind and had got his sight, until they called the parents of the one who had gained his sight, and questioned them, saying, "Is this your son, of whom you say that he was born blind? How then does he now see?" His parents answered them and said, "We know that this is our son, and that he was born blind; but how he sees we do not know, or who opened his eyes we ourselves do not know. Ask him; he is of age, let him speak for himself." These things his parents said because they feared the Jews. For already the Jews had agreed that if anyone were to confess him to be the Christ, he should be put out of the synagogue. This is why his parents said, "He is of age; question him."

They therefore called a second time the man who had been blind, and said to him, "Give glory to God! We ourselves know that this man is a sinner." He therefore said, "Whether he is a sinner, I do not know. One thing I do know, that whereas I was blind, now I see." They therefore said to him, "What did he do to thee? How did he open thy eyes?" He answered them, "I have told you already, and you have heard. Why would you hear again? Would you also become his disciples?" They heaped abuse on him therefore, and said, "Thou art his disciple, but we are disciples of Moses. We know that God spoke to Moses; but as for this man we do not know where he is from." In answer the man said to them, "Why, herein is the marvel, that you do not know where he is from, and yet he opened my eyes. Now we know that God does not hear sinners; but if anyone is a worshipper of God, and does his will, him he hears. Not from the beginning of the world has it been heard that anyone opened the eyes of a man born blind. If this man were not from God, he could do nothing." They answered and said to him, "Thou wast altogether born in sins, and dost thou teach us?" And they turned him out.

Jesus heard that they had turned him out, and when he had found him, said to him, "Dost thou believe in the Son of God?" He answered and said, "Who is he, Lord, that I may believe in him?" And Jesus said to him, "Thou hast both seen him, and he it is who speaks with thee." And he said, "I believe, Lord." And falling down, he worshipped him" (John 9:18–38).

This was the miracle of the granting of sight to the man born blind. It was something that could not be explained on natural grounds. Yet the Pharisees stubbornly refused to believe, while the humble blind man in the face of personal danger confessed Christ to be God. The miracle actually happened; it was carefully verified by hostile witnesses; it was offered by Christ as a proof of His divinity.

Raising the dead to life. The Gospels mention three persons whom Christ raised from the dead to life: the daughter of Jairus (Matthew 9:18–26; Mark 5:21–43); the widow's son of Naim (Luke 7:11–17); and Lazarus (John 11:1–44). By far the greatest of Christ's miracles was His own Resurrection from the dead. The Resurrection is of such importance for establishing the truth of Christianity that it warrants separate and special treatment. At this time it will be profitable for us to consider at some length the raising of Lazarus from the dead because of the circumstances of this miracle, the large number of witnesses, and the fact that Christ publicly appealed to His heavenly Father and asked that this miracle be in proof of His divine mission.

THE RAISING OF LAZARUS. Lazarus of Bethany, the brother of Mary and Martha, was a friend of Jesus. So when he was taken seriously ill, the sisters sent word to Jesus, saying, "*Lord, behold, he whom thou lovest is sick.*" Despite this message, Jesus remained two more days in the place where the message reached Him, before telling His disciples that Lazarus was dead and that they would go to him in Judea.

So then Jesus said to them plainly, "Lazarus is dead; and I rejoice on your account that I was not there, that you may believe. But let us go to him. . . .

Jesus therefore came and found him already four days in the tomb. Now Bethany was close to Jerusalem, some fifteen stadia distant. And many of the Jews had come to Martha and Mary, to comfort them on account of their brother. When, therefore, Martha heard that Jesus was coming, she went to meet him. But Mary remained at home.

Martha therefore said to Jesus, "Lord, if thou hadst been here my brother would not have died. But even now I know that whatever thou shalt ask of God, God will give it to thee." Jesus said to her, "Thy brother shall rise." Martha said to him, "I know that he will rise at the resurrection, on the last day." Jesus said to her, "I am the resurrection and the life; he who believes in me, even if he die, shall live; and whoever lives and believes in me, shall never die. Dost thou believe this?" She said to him, "Yes, Lord, I believe that thou art the Christ, the Son of God, who hast come into the world."

And when she had said this, she went away and quietly called Mary her sister, saying, "The Master is here and calls thee." As soon as she heard this, she rose quickly and came to him, for Jesus had not yet come into the village, but was still at the place where Martha had met him. When, therefore, the Jews who were with her in the house and were comforting her, saw Mary rise up quickly and go out, they followed her, saying, "She is going to the tomb to weep there."

When, therefore, Mary came where Jesus was, and saw him, she fell at his feet, and said to him, "Lord, if thou hadst been here, my brother would not have died." When, therefore, Jesus saw her weeping, and the Jews who had come with her weeping, he groaned in spirit and was troubled, and said, "Where have you laid him?" They said to him, "Lord, come and see." And Jesus wept. The Jews therefore said, "See how he loved him." But some of them said, "Could not he who opened the eyes of the blind, have caused that this man should not die?"

Jesus therefore, again groaning in himself, came to the tomb. Now it was a cave, and a stone was laid against it. Jesus said, "Take away the stone." Martha, the sister of him who was dead, said to him, "Lord, by this time he is already decayed, for he is dead four days." Jesus said to her, "Have I not told thee that if thou believe thou shalt behold the glory of God?" They therefore removed the stone. And Jesus, raising his eyes, said, "Father, I give thee thanks that thou hast heard me. Yet I knew that thou always hearest me; but because of the people who stand round, I spoke, that they may believe that thou hast sent me." When he had said this, he cried out with a loud voice, "Lazarus, come forth!" And at once he who had been dead came forth, bound feet and hands with bandages, and his face was tied up with a cloth. Jesus said to them, "Unbind him and let him go."

Many therefore of the Jews who had come to Mary, and had seen what he did, believed in him. But some of them went away to the Pharisees, and told them the things that Jesus had done (John 11:14–46).

We selected for brief consideration only two of the many wonderful miracles which Christ performed. It is difficult to see how these two miracles could possibly be explained away since the circumstances of each are such that every conceivable objection seems to have been anticipated. The enemies of Christ are hard put to discount His miracles since they are so numerous and so varied, so spectacular and so public. Unless these enemies can do a complete job they have failed. One clearcut miracle is all that is necessary to prove Christ's claim to be divine.

Now Jesus performed His many miracles, not merely as the representative or ambassador of God, but as God Himself: *"If I do not perform the works [miracles] of my Father, do not believe me. But if I do perform them, and if you are not willing to believe me, believe the works, that you may know and believe that the Father is in me and I in the Father" (John 10:37–38).*

REVIEW QUESTIONS

1 Why is the proof of Christ's divinity called the most important proof in apologetics?

2 Why do we say that God must have placed the sign of His approval on Christ in such a way that no reasonable man who examines the evidence can deny His divinity?

3 What kinds of evidence must be looked for to justify Christ's claim to be God?

4 Briefly outline the nature and scope of the internal evidence to prove Christ's claim.

5 What is *character,* and on what basis do we make judgments about one's character?

6 What is meant by saying that Christ's character is sublime?
7 Briefly outline the nature of the external evidence required to justify Christ's claim to be God.
8 What is meant by saying that Christ's teachings are sublime?
9 How can we show that Christ's personal life was above reproach?
10 What is a miracle?
11 Have we an accurate record of the miracles of Christ?
12 What kinds of miracles are mentioned in the Gospels?
13 Since we do not know everything that nature can do, is it not possible that Christ's miracles may eventually be explained away when we have learned more about the laws of nature?
14 How many miracles are necessary to prove that Christ's claim to divinity is true?
15 What circumstances make the cure of the man born blind a well-attested and important miracle in proof of the divinity of Christ?
16 What is notable about the miracle of raising Lazarus from the dead?

SUGGESTIONS FOR READING

"Miracles," *Things Catholics Are Asked About*, Martin J. Scott, S.J. New York: P. J. Kenedy & Sons, 1927, Chapter V, pp. 34–41.

Christ, the Wonder-Worker, Richard Ginder. Catholic Information Society, 214 West 31st Street, New York 1, N.Y. 14 pp., 5¢. (No one denies that Christ worked miracles, but many try to explain them away.)

God's Signature, Richard Ginder. Catholic Information Society. 14 pp., 5¢. (Miracles are a sign of God's approval.)

The Kindness of God, James Walsh, C.S.P. The Paulist Press, 401 West 59th Street, New York 19, N.Y., 1959. 32 pp., 10¢. (Christ's outstanding human qualities, His miracles, His sublime teachings, His acts of divinity.)

Reni photo

"*Christ in Majesty*" is the title of the mosaic pictured above, which covers the inner wall of the north apse of the National Shrine of the Immaculate Conception, Washington, D.C. The face of Christ is eight feet high and five feet wide. The mosaic uses four thousand shades of color.

Chapter 11

Christ proved His claims, II

IN THE PRECEDING chapter we considered the miracles of Christ in proof of His claim to be divine. We asserted that one well-attested miracle alone would be sufficient to prove that Christ was what He claimed to be; the true Son of God. However, we were able to cite not one, but many well-attested miracles of various kinds to make the proof of Christ's claim all the more impressive.

Let it not be thought that we have exhausted the proofs that can be brought forward to prove the divinity of Christ.

We are now ready to consider another method of proof, namely, evidence of the part played by prophecies in the life of Christ. Here again we shall find an abundance of examples to draw upon.

Finally we shall consider that event in Christ's life which is the crowning proof of His divinity—an event which is both an outstanding miracle and the fulfillment of prophecies—Christ's Resurrection from the dead.

The Role of Prophecies

Only God can foresee with certainty a future event involving the free action of God or man. Therefore the certain and definite prediction of such an event requires either divine knowledge or divine assistance. This is what we call prophecy. Without help from God no mere man can utter a prophecy. It is, of course, not prophecy when the weather bureau predicts that we are going to have a storm or a cold spell within a matter of hours or days. These weather experts base their forecasts on known laws and past experience. Neither is it prophecy when an astronomer predicts an eclipse of the sun, even months or years in advance. He bases his prediction on his knowledge of natural laws and his ability to make the necessary mathematical calculations. Men with the requisite knowledge or skills are able to predict many things that are due to natural or social forces without passing into the realm of prophecy as we have defined it.

Now prophecies have an important role in proving that Christ's claim to divinity was true. Christ was Himself the fulfillment of prophecies made centuries before His birth which must have been revealed by God. Christ also uttered many prophecies Himself, which were fulfilled either during His lifetime on earth or afterwards. These prophecies concerned Himself or His disciples or they referred to Jerusalem and the Jewish people or the Church which He was to establish. From these prophecies we argue that Christ was either

God or had upon Him the seal of God's approval which would confirm His claim to divinity. It is worthy of note that on more than one occasion Christ mentioned that the prophets of the Old Testament had written concerning Him. Also, when predicting the treason of Judas, Christ said: *"I tell you now before it comes to pass, that when it has come to pass you may believe that I am he" (John 13:19).*

Christ Himself the fulfillment of prophecy. The religion of the Jews was a religion of expectation, with the belief in a Messias or a Redeemer to come as one of its chief doctrines. The sacred books of the Jews, which now make up the Old Testament in our Catholic Bible (to distinguish it from the New Testament, which contains the Four Gospels and other documents of Christianity), contain numerous prophecies about the Redeemer. All that had been foretold of this Redeemer was accurately fulfilled in Christ. We can do no more than give a brief summary of some of the important items with the citations from the Old Testament so that the prophecies can be read in their context.

A description of the Redeemer as compiled from prophecies in the Old Testament reads as follows: He will be descended from David (Isaias 11:1–2), and will be born at Bethlehem (Micheas 5:2). He will be born of a virgin mother (Isaias 7:14). He will be called the Son of God (Psalms 2:7). He will reside for a time in Egypt (Osee 11:1). Prophetic details of Christ's passion and death and the attainment of His mission are particularly noteworthy. Thus, His Palm Sunday entrance into Jerusalem is mentioned (Zacharias 9:9). He will be sold for thirty pieces of silver, and the silver will be used to purchase the potter's field (Zacharias 11:12–13). He will be offered of His own accord, and will not open His mouth; He will be led as sheep to the slaughter, and will be dumb as a lamb before His shearer (Isaias 53:7). His disciples will flee when He is taken prisoner (Zacharias 13:7). His hands and feet will be pierced, His garments will be divided and lots cast upon His vesture (Psalm 21:17–19). They will give Him gall and vinegar to drink (Psalm 68:22). He will judge all men and crown the just with glory (Isaias 24, 28). He will be a light to the Gentiles and bring salvation to the ends of the earth (Isaias 49:6). The God of Heaven will set up a kingdom that shall never be destroyed (Daniel 2:44).

Christ's prophecies about Himself. Christ foretold clearly His Passion (Matthew 20:18–19), His Resurrection (Matthew 26:32, 27:63), His Ascension (John 6:63).

Christ's prophecies about His disciples. He foretold that Judas would betray Him (Matthew 26:21–25); that Peter would deny Him (Mark 14:30; Matthew 26:34); that all His disciples would forsake Him (Mark 14:27; Matthew 26:31); that His apostles would suffer persecution (Matthew 10: 17–18).

Christ's prophecies about Jerusalem and the Jews. He said: *"For days will come upon thee when thy enemies will throw up a rampart about thee, and surround thee and shut thee in on every side, and will dash thee to the ground and thy children within thee, and will not leave in thee one stone upon another, because thou hast not known the time of thy visitation" (Luke 19:43–44).* And again: *"When you see Jerusalem being surrounded by an army, then know that her desolation is at hand. . . . For there will be great distress over the land, and wrath upon this people. And they will fall by the edge of the sword, and will be led away as captives to all the nations. And Jerusalem will be trodden down by the Gentiles, until the times of the nations be fulfilled" (Luke 21:20–24).*

The *History of the Jewish War,* written by the Jewish historian, Flavius Josephus (A.D. 37–98), reveals how accurately these prophecies were fulfilled in the war waged against the Jews. The complete destruction of Jerusalem and the temple in 70 A.D. was quite unexpected, as it was the usual Roman practice to preserve conquered cities and particularly the temples.

Christ's prophecies about His Church. He foretold that His Church would grow like the mustard seed (Matthew 13: 31–32); that it would leaven all mankind (Matthew 13:33); that, like Himself, it would be persecuted by the world (Matthew 10:17–18); but that it would not fail and the gates of hell would not prevail against it (Matthew 16:18) because He would be with His Church all days, even to the consummation of the world (Matthew 28:20).

The Resurrection of Christ

The Resurrection of Christ has been reserved for special treatment as the crowning proof of Christ's divinity because it is by far the greatest of Christ's miracles. Moreover, it was in itself the fulfillment of a prophecy. Christ claimed to be God. In proof of His claim He said that He would rise from the dead. If Christ rose from the dead, His claim to divinity is true and therefore Christ is God.

The miracle of Resurrection is the keystone of Christianity, not merely because of the kind of miracle it is in itself, but chiefly because Christ Himself foretold it would happen and put emphasis upon it. The apostle St. Paul says of the Resurrection, *"If Christ has not risen, vain then is our preaching, vain too is your faith" (I Corinthians 15:14).* St. Augustine says that had not the Resurrection been a fact, the conversion of the world to belief in it by a few Galilean fishermen would have been as great a miracle as the Resurrection itself (*The City of God,* Book xxii, Ch. V).

The circumstances of Christ's death and Resurrection are such that they seem to anticipate and provide ready answers to the objections that have been raised from time to time by unbelievers. The Resurrection can be demonstrated as true beyond any reasonable doubt.

Christ's promise that He would rise from the dead. When the Jews demanded a miracle in proof of His authority, Christ answered: *"Destroy this temple and in three days I will raise* *it up"* (*John 2:19*). *"He was speaking,"* the evangelist says, *"of the temple of his body."* Later He speaks more clearly: *"An evil and adulterous generation demands a sign, and no sign shall be given it but the sign of Jonas the prophet. For even as Jonas was in the belly of the fish three days and three nights, so will the Son of Man be three days and three nights in the heart of the earth"* (*Matthew 12:39–40*). After the transfiguration, He said to Peter, James, and John: *"Tell the vision to no one, till the Son of Man has risen from the dead"* (*Matthew 17:9*). Before going up to Jerusalem to suffer, He said with perfect distinctness: *"Behold, we are going up to Jerusalem, and the Son of Man will be betrayed to the chief priests and the Scribes; and they will condemn him to death, and will deliver him to the Gentiles to be mocked and scourged and crucified; and on the third day he will rise again"* (*Matthew 20:18–19*). That He had foretold His Resurrection was well known to all, for the Jews, after His death, said to Pilate: *"We have remembered how that deceiver said, while he was yet alive, 'After three days I will rise again' "* (*Matthew 27:63*).

Christ's death and burial. There can be no doubt about the fact that Christ died upon the cross. For no other historical personage is there more certain evidence about the circumstances and manner of death and burial than there is for Christ. It would seem that the evidence available is of a character to nullify every attempt of the enemies of Christianity to explain away Christ's death. In fact, their possible objections seem to have been anticipated.

Previous to the actual crucifixion, Christ had already been greatly weakened by the bloody agony in the Garden of Olives, by the savage scourging, by the cruel crowning with thorns, and by other mistreatment meted out to Him from the moment He was seized in the Garden until He arrived on Calvary for crucifixion. From a physical point of view, it is remarkable that Christ ever reached Calvary, so weak and exhausted was He. In fact, His Roman executioners felt it necessary to draft the Cyrenian, Simon, to assist their Victim with His cross lest He die on the way. So the wonder is, not that Christ died on the Cross only three hours after He was nailed to it, but that His human endurance could last that long.

We have the testimony of the four evangelists, who say clearly that Christ died on the cross. St. Matthew tells us that: *Jesus again cried out with a loud voice, and gave up his spirit (Matthew 27:50).* The three other evangelists likewise declare that Jesus died (Mark 15:37; Luke 23:46; John 19:30). When the Roman centurion who was keeping guard over Jesus, *saw how he had thus cried out and expired, he [the centurion] said, "Truly this man was the Son of God" (Mark 15:39).* At the request of the Jews, Pilate sent soldiers to break the legs of the victims so that they could be removed from the crosses before the Sabbath. *The soldiers therefore came and broke the legs of the first, and of the other, who had been crucified with him. But when they came to Jesus, and saw that he was already dead, they did not break his legs; but one of the soldiers opened his side with a lance, and immediately there came out blood and water (John 19:32–34).*

Furthermore, Joseph of Arimathea went to Pilate to ask for the body of Jesus: *But Pilate wondered whether he had already died. And sending for the centurion, he asked him whether he was already dead. And when he learned from the centurion that he was, he granted the body to Joseph. And Joseph bought a linen cloth, and took him down, and wrapped him in the linen cloth, and laid him in a tomb which had been hewn out of a rock (Mark 15:44–46).* There was, of course, no likelihood that the enemies of Jesus would leave their work unfinished. As a matter of fact, the chief priests and the Pharisees went in a body to Pilate, saying, "*Sir, we have remembered how that deceiver said, while he was yet alive, 'After three days I will rise again.' Give orders, therefore, that the sepulchre be guarded until the third day, or else his disciples may come and steal him away, and say to the people*

'He has risen from the dead'; and the last imposture will be worse than the first." Pilate said to them, "You have a guard; go, guard it as well as you know how." So they went and made the sepulchre secure, sealing the stone, and setting the guard (Matthew 27:63–66).

The evidence of Christ's death and burial as found in the Four Gospels could hardly be clearer in showing that Christ's death was known and admitted by all, disciples, enemies, and the Romans. The Roman historian Tacitus, who lived from about 55 to 120 A.D., says that "Christus was put to death by the procurator, Pontius Pilate, in the reign of Tiberius" (*Annals* xv, 44). The cross, which has come down to us through the centuries as the revered symbol of Christianity, is of itself eloquent testimony to the unwavering conviction of millions that Christ died on the cross on Good Friday almost two thousand years ago.

Christ's Resurrection from the dead. The evidence for Christ's Resurrection from the dead is no less convincing than the evidence for His death. We have already mentioned Christ's positive prediction of His Resurrection (Matthew 20:19) and the fact that His prediction was generally known, as indicated by the request of the high priests and the Pharisees that Pilate set a guard about the tomb (Matthew 27:63–64).

All four of the evangelists tell us of the Resurrection of Christ: St. Matthew in Chapter 28, St. Mark in Chapter 16, St. Luke in Chapter 24, and St. John in Chapter 20. By way of example, we cite here the account of St. John because he described what he saw with his own eyes: *Now on the first day of the week, Mary Magdalene came early to the tomb, while it was still dark, and she saw the stone taken away from the tomb. She ran therefore and came to Simon Peter, and to the other disciple whom Jesus loved, and said to them, "They have taken the Lord from the tomb, and we do not know where they have laid him."*

Peter therefore went out, and the other disciple, and they went to the tomb. The two were running together, and the other disciple ran on before, faster than Peter, and came first to the tomb. And stooping down he saw the linen cloths lying there, yet he did not enter. Simon Peter therefore came following him, and he went into the tomb, and saw the linen cloths lying there, and the handkerchief which had been about his head, not lying with the linen cloths, but folded in a place by itself. Then the other disciple also went in, who had come first to the tomb. And he saw and believed; for as yet they did not understand the Scripture, that he must rise from the dead. The disciples therefore went away again to their home (John 20: 1–10).

After He arose from the dead Christ remained on earth until He publicly ascended into Heaven, as He had also foretold (John 6:63), forty days after His Resurrection. During that time Christ appeared frequently to individuals and to groups, even large groups. On one occasion, He was seen by more than five hundred brethren at once (I Corinthians 15:6). On these occasions Christ spoke and even ate with His disciples; He permitted them to examine His wounds; and He repeatedly declared that He had indeed risen from the dead.

Thus, for example, Christ appeared to Mary Magdalene and the other women (Matthew 28:9–10). He appeared to two disciples on their way to Emmaus (Luke 24:13–32). He appeared to the eleven in Jerusalem (two separate occasions are mentioned: Luke 24:36–43 and John 20:26). He appeared to several of the apostles at the sea of Tiberius (John 21:1–23). We will quote only the text of the gospel account of Christ's first appearance at Jerusalem to His apostles (all but Thomas).

Now while they were talking of these things, Jesus stood in their midst, and said to them, "Peace to you! It is I, do not be afraid." But they were startled and panic-stricken, and thought that they saw a spirit.

And he said to them, "Why are you disturbed, and why do doubts arise in your hearts? See my hands and feet, that it is I myself. Feel me and see; for a spirit does not have flesh and bones, as you see I have." And having said this, he showed them his hands and his feet. But as they still disbelieved and marveled for joy, he said, "Have you anything here to eat?" And they offered him a piece of broiled fish and a honeycomb. And when he had eaten in their presence, he took what remained and gave it to them (Luke 24:36–43).

The historical gospel records certainly show that there was no dearth of evidence or witnesses to prove that Christ truly arose from the dead. The rationalists and the enemies of Christianity have been hard pressed in trying to disprove the truth of the Resurrection. They have tried to discredit the witnesses by suggesting that they were victims of hallucination. These unbelievers point out that the followers of Christ were in a state of nervous excitement after the crucifixion; they believed that their beloved Master would triumph over the grave and come back to them again. Their wishful thinking and their highly emotional longing for His return brought forth the fancied vision of the risen Saviour. This theory might seem plausible to one who has not carefully examined the evidence, but when all the evidence is considered, the theory is completely demolished. That an individual might suffer such a hallucination is possible; that all the apostles and hundreds of the disciples should suffer from the same hallucination simultaneously and over a long period is impossible. The evidence against this "wishful thinking and highly emotional longing" is devastating. The followers of Christ were not expecting His Resurrection, even though Christ had foretold it to them (Matthew 16:21–22). It was very difficult to convince them that He had actually risen from the dead (Luke 24:10–11, 25). Thus Mary Magdalene and the other women brought spices to embalm His body on the morning of the third day. They certainly did not expect to find Him risen from the dead (Mark 16:1–6). Mary Magdalene's first thought, when she saw the empty tomb, was that someone had stolen the body (John 20:1–2). The apostles refused to believe that

Christ had risen from the dead either on the report of Mary Magdalene to whom Christ appeared or the report of the two disciples who met Him on the road to Emmaus (Mark 16:11–13). The reaction of the apostle Thomas to the word of all the other apostles that the Lord had appeared to them during his absence is well known. *"Unless I see in his hands the print of the nails, and put my finger into the place of the nails, and put my hand into his side, I will not believe" (John 20:25).* There can be no doubt about it, the witnesses to the risen Christ were not subject to hallucinations. They were mostly a hardheaded lot who were more inclined to be incredulous than credulous. They merited, for the most part, the gentle rebuke of Christ addressed to the "doubting" Thomas. *"Bring here thy finger and see my hands; and bring here thy hand, and put it into my side; and be not unbelieving, but believing" (John 20:27).*

Supplementary proofs. In all our arguments and proofs we have limited ourselves to the historical evidence of the Four Gospels. If we turn to the equally historical document, called the *Acts of the Apostles,* which takes up where the Gospels leave off and gives us a history of the early Church, we have additional evidence to confirm the truth of the Resurrection. (St. Luke, who wrote the third Gospel, also wrote the *Acts.* The same tests which proved his Gospel to be a genuine historical document also apply to the *Acts of the Apostles.*)

THE TEACHING OF THE APOSTLES CONFIRMED BY MIRACLES. When the apostles received the Holy Spirit on Pentecost Sunday, ten days after the Ascension of our Lord into heaven and fifty days after His Resurrection, they began their mission of preaching the risen Christ and propagating His teachings. Through the apostles and in the name of the risen Christ, God wrought many signs and wonders to put the seal of His approval upon the truths which the apostles preached. We note in particular the miracle of tongues (Acts 2:6–7), the cure of the man lame from birth (Acts 3:1–11), the deliverance of the apostles from prison (Acts 5:18–23).

WORLD-WIDE BELIEF IN THE RESURRECTION. When the apostles began their mission on Pentecost, they spoke boldly of the Resurrection of Christ. On this, the birthday of the Church, three thousand Jews were converted by St. Peter to belief in Christ whom, he said, *"God hath raised up, and we are all witnesses of it" (Acts 2:32).* Five thousand more converts were added a few days later when Peter spoke of Christ as *"the author of life you killed, whom God has raised up from the dead; whereof we are witnesses" (Acts 3:15; 4:4).* From Jerusalem, throughout Palestine, and beyond, converts of every rank and race increased rapidly. Within a few years Christians were counted by hundred thousands. Within a few centuries, they were numbered by the millions. It is a continuous miracle of belief which becomes more and more impressive as the centuries pass. Within the Church today, there are five hundred million believers, and approximately three hundred thirty million outside the Church who profess belief in Christ. Among these believers are men of every race and class and degree of intelligence, including many of the world's most learned men. Well does St. Augustine say that had not the Resurrection been a fact, the conversion of the world to belief in it by a few Galilean fishermen would have been as great a miracle as the Resurrection itself. Thus does God show that His apostles spoke the truth in saying that Christ, our Lord, really rose from the dead.

Without doubt, the historical person, Jesus Christ, was more than an ordinary man, more even than a special envoy or ambassador from God. He was, as Peter confessed on at least two occasions, *"the Christ, the Son of the living God" (Matthew 16:17).*

REVIEW QUESTIONS

1 What is a prophecy?
2 Why are the long-range predictions of such phenomena as eclipses of the sun, the emergence of storms, cold spells, etc., not considered to be prophecies?
3 Why is a prophecy considered to be a sign of God's approval?

4 What bearing do prophecies have upon Christ's claim to be the Son of God?
5 What kinds of prophecies are used in proving Christ's divinity?
6 Give two examples of prophecies that were fulfilled in Christ.
7 Give two examples of Christ's prophecies about Himself.
8 Give two examples of Christ's prophecies about His disciples.
9 Give two examples of Christ's prophecies about His Church.
10 Give an example of Christ's prophecy about Jerusalem.
11 Why is so much importance attached to Christ's Resurrection from the dead?
12 Why is the Resurrection of Christ called the keystone of Christianity?
13 Give one gospel quotation showing Christ's prediction of His Resurrection.
14 What evidence have we for Christ's death and burial?
15 What evidence do we have for Christ's Resurrection from the dead?
16 After His Resurrection, how long did Christ remain on earth?
17 Beginning on the first Pentecost the apostles boldly preached Christ crucified and risen from the dead. How can this be turned into an argument for the truth of Christ's Resurrection?
18 How can the current world-wide diffusion of belief in the Resurrection be used as an argument to prove the truth of the Resurrection?

SUGGESTIONS FOR READING

"The Resurrection," *Things Catholics Are Asked About,* Martin J. Scott, S.J. New York: P. J. Kenedy & Sons, 1927, Chapter IV, pp. 24–34.

History's Greatest Build-up, Richard Ginder. Catholic Information Society, 214 West 31st Street, New York 1, N.Y. 16 pp., 5¢. (Christ was the fulfillment of many prophecies stretching back for thousands of years.)

The Facts Behind the Resurrection, Richard Ginder. Catholic Information Society, 15 pp., 5¢. (Jesus predicted His own Resurrection; His enemies understood these predictions; there were many witnesses of the Resurrection.)

Jesus Christ: God and Man! Wilfred G. Hurley, C.S.P. The Paulist Press, 1934. 24 pp., 10¢. (Testifies to the truth of the Old Testament and then shows that prophecies, miracles, and finally the Resurrection prove that Christ was both God and Man.)

The Third Day, Arnold Lunn. Westminster, Md.: Newman Press, 1945. 177 pp. (A modern popular exposition of the reality of the central event of Christianity, the Resurrection.)

FPG photo

Christ's command to His apostles, "*Go into the whole world and preach the Gospel to every creature*" *(Mark 16:15)*, is still being observed even in the remotest areas of the world. In the picture above tribesmen in the Far East are being instructed in Christianity.

Chapter **12**

Christ founded a Church

Universality of Christ's Mission

WE HAVE PROVED TO OUR complete satisfaction that Jesus Christ is not only God's accredited messenger with a great new revelation for mankind, but also that He is actually the Son of God. Christ is the long-promised Redeemer who came into the world to save men from sin and to restore them to the friendship of God. His mission was to the whole human race and not merely to the Jewish people.

Christ spent only three years of His life on earth as the

teacher and "wonder worker" in Palestine, a comparatively small area of the then-known world. But during that time, as we intend to demonstrate from the Gospels, He founded an organization to carry on the work He had begun and to make known to all men the revelation which He came on earth to bring.

A Visible Society to Continue Christ's Work

The essential requirement for a visible society is that it unite together a number of persons for some common purpose to be attained by common means and under a common authority. It is very clear from the Gospels that Christ did establish such a visible organization or society with these essential qualifications. However, His organization was a religious society, or Church, because it was dedicated especially to the service of God. Nevertheless, it was a real society because it banded together a number of persons to do the will of God by professing the same beliefs, by worshipping God in the same way under the authority of the same lawfully constituted leaders. One does not have to search through the Gospels very long before uncovering sufficient evidence to prove this and to identify these four essentials in the society which Christ established and which He called His Church.

Followers gathered. It is evident from the beginning of Christ's public life that He encouraged men to follow Him and to remain with Him constantly, and that upon these men He bestowed the most careful instruction: *"Come, follow me, and I will make you fishers of men" (Mark 1:17).* He gathered others around Him and gave them specific work to do: *The Lord appointed seventy-two others, and sent them forth two by two before him into every town and place where he himself was about to come. And he said to them, "The harvest is indeed great, but the laborers are few. Pray therefore the Lord of the harvest to send forth laborers into his harvest" (Luke 10:1–2).*

A common goal. The purpose of the society which Christ called into being was the same purpose for which He Himself had come into the world, namely, to cleanse men from sin, to make them holy, and to make them children of God and heirs of heaven. "*As the Father has sent me, I also send you*" (*John 20:21*). "*He who does the will of my Father in heaven shall enter the kingdom of heaven*" (*Matthew 7:21*). "*Seek the kingdom of God, and all these things shall be given you besides*" (*Luke 12:31*). "*Whosoever does not accept the kingdom of God as a little child will not enter into it*" (*Luke 18:17*).

Means to achievement. It was Christ Himself who gave to His Church the common means by which salvation was to be attained. He gave His Church the doctrines to be believed, the commandments to be obeyed, and the sacred rites to be made use of. "*Go into the whole world and preach the gospel to every creature. He who believes and is baptized shall be saved, but he who does not believe shall be condemned*" (*Mark 16:15–16*). "*If thou wilt enter into life, keep the commandments*" (*Matthew 19:17*). "*If anyone love me, he will keep my word, and my Father will love him, and we will come to him and make our abode with him*" (*John 14:23*). "*Amen, amen, I say to thee, unless a man be born again of water and the Spirit, he cannot enter into the kingdom of God*" (*John 3:5*). "*God is spirit, and they who worship him must worship in spirit and in truth*" (*John 4:24*).

A common authority. It was Christ Himself who gave the government of the Church its authority, its right to require obedience of all its members. The apostles were not sent to act independently of one another, but to govern by their collective authority under Peter as their head. "*Thou art Peter, and upon this rock I will build my Church, and the gates of hell shall not prevail against it. And I will give thee the keys of the kingdom of heaven; and whatever thou shalt bind on earth shall be bound in heaven, and whatever thou shalt loose on earth shall be loosed in heaven*" (*Matthew 16:18–20*). "*Go,* *therefore, and make disciples of all nations, baptizing them in the name of the Father, and of the Son, and of the Holy Spirit, teaching them to observe all that I have commanded you; and behold, I am with you all days, even unto the consummation of the world" (Matthew 28:19–20). "He who hears you, hears me; and he who rejects you, rejects me; and he who rejects me, rejects him who sent me" (Luke 10:16).*

St. Peter Made Head of Church

It is abundantly clear from the Gospels that Simon Peter held a position of pre-eminence among the apostles, and regularly acted as their spokesman. Thus, on the occasions when Christ asked His disciples, "*Who do men say the Son of Man is?" (Matthew 16:13)* and, "*Do you also wish to go away?" (John 6:68)*, Simon Peter answered in the name of all, "*Thou art the Christ, the Son of God" (Matthew 16:16; John 6:70).* On another occasion, when Christ foretold His forthcoming passion, death and resurrection, Peter took it upon himself to remonstrate with our Lord, saying, "*Far be it from thee, O Lord; this will never happen to thee" (Matthew 16:22).* Although Peter was rebuked for this impetuous statement, the example seems to show that Peter considered himself to be Christ's chief assistant.

Christ Himself gave pre-eminence to Simon Peter. Thus, whenever Christ selected a group of the apostles for any special purpose, Peter was always one of the group (Mark 1: 36). Peter it was who was sent to the sea to take from the fish a miraculous coin to pay the tax collector "*for me and for thee" (Matthew 17:26).* It probably was no great surprise to the apostles when Christ publicly, in their presence, made Peter the head of the Church. "*Thou art Peter, and upon this rock I will build my Church, and the gates of hell shall not prevail against it. And I will give thee the keys of the kingdom of heaven; and whatever thou shalt bind on earth shall be bound in heaven, and whatever thou shalt loose on earth shall be loosed in heaven" (Matthew 16:18–19).* This promise was confirmed by Christ after His Resurrection, when He entrusted to Peter the flock which He Himself was about to leave (John 21:15:17). After His Resurrection Christ appeared to Peter alone before appearing to all the apostles (Luke 24:34).

St. Peter acted as head. After Christ ascended into heaven Peter was functioning as the leader and head of the newborn Church. It was he who presided at the choosing of Matthias to take the place of Judas (Acts 1:15). It was Peter who, after receiving the Holy Spirit on Pentecost day, first preached Christ crucified to the Jews and received three thousand converts into the new Church (Acts 2:14–41). It was Peter who worked the first miracle on the lame beggar at the gate of the temple and took advantage of the occasion to preach again to the Jews and to explain that the lame man was cured by means of faith in the name of Jesus Christ (Acts 3:1–26). On at least two occasions when St. Peter and one or more of the other apostles were arrested by the Jews for preaching Jesus, it was Peter who boldly faced the Jewish interrogators and answered in the name of all (Acts 4:8, 5:29). St. Peter was the one who passed sentence on Ananias (Acts 5:3). It was St. Peter who decided that the Gentiles should be admitted to the Church (Acts 10:48), and decreed later that they should not be required to observe the precepts of the Jewish law (Acts 15: 7–12).

St. Peter recognized as head. After Christ's Resurrection the angel sent a special message to Peter by the holy women (Mark 16:7). Although arriving at the tomb first, the apostle John, out of respect for Peter, waited for him to go first into the empty sepulchre (John 20:5). The evangelists always list Peter's name first whenever mentioning it along with the names of other apostles. *First Simon, who is called Peter (Matthew 10:2).* The regularity of this recurring mention of St. Peter in the first place whenever a group of apostles are mentioned is additional evidence that he held a primacy of honor and jurisdiction. There is no record or hint that any of the other apostles or any of the early Christians ever questioned the headship of St. Peter. We have as great, if not greater, certitude that he was the first head of Christ's Church as we have that George Washington was the first president of the United States.

From the arguments which we have considered at length there seems to be no reason to doubt that Christ founded a Church and appointed Peter as its head.

Permanency of Church

Christ intended His Church to be permanent. He promised, *"I am with you all days, even unto the consummation of the world" (Matthew 28:20)*, and *"the gates of hell shall not prevail against it" (Matthew 16:18)*. These are definite promises which mean that Christ's Church will endure until the end of time and that Christ will protect it from such dangers as might destroy it.

Furthermore, the mission which Christ gave to His apostles was such that it could not be accomplished in their lifetime, has not been accomplished up to the present and, in fact, cannot be fully accomplished until the end of the world. *"Go into the whole world and preach the gospel to every creature. He who believes and is baptized shall be saved, but he who does not believe shall be condemned" (Mark 16:15–16)*.

The Bishop of Rome, successor of St. Peter. If Christ's Church is to last until the end of time as He clearly promised, He must have intended that St. Peter and the apostles would be succeeded by others upon their deaths. Thus there must exist in the world today someone who is the true successor of St. Peter.

Now history testifies that St. Peter, the first head of the Church, was also Bishop of Rome, and that he died there and was buried there. History also testifies that the Bishop of Rome has always been looked upon as the lawful successor of St. Peter. This is evident from the testimony of the very earliest writers, such as St. Ignatius the Martyr, who died about 117 A.D., and St. Irenaeus, who died in the year 202 A.D. The writings of the fathers of the Church are also sources testifying to the supreme authority of the Bishop of Rome. Furthermore, the bishops of Rome have always claimed and exercised supreme authority over the Church, whereas no one else claims or has claimed to wield this authority. The earliest councils of the Church recognized the authority of the Roman pontiff. From the very earliest times there are on record instances of matters of faith having been submitted to the Roman pontiff for authoritative decision, but no record whatever of any bishop of Rome submitting to the judgment or decision of anyone else concerning matters of faith.

Finally, ancient Christian art bears witness by frequently representing the Roman pontiff, in some form or other, as the successor of St. Peter and the chief pastor of the flock of Christ.

According to Catholic teaching it is the Bishop of Rome who is the successor of St. Peter, the vicar of Christ on earth, and the visible head of the Church. Knowing this, Protestant reformers and rationalists have tried to cast doubt on the tradition that St. Peter was Bishop of Rome, that he lived for a time at Rome, that he suffered martyrdom there, and was buried there. A few opponents have even ventured to assert that Peter was never in Rome. The purpose of all this has been to undermine the papacy, which attaches great importance to the belief that St. Peter lived, died and was buried in Rome. However, the accumulation of historical and archaeological evidence has been so great that no reputable scholar today questions Peter's sojourn, martyr's death, and burial in Rome.

According to tradition, St. Peter was crucified head downward in a pagan cemetery on Vatican hill outside the walls of Rome about 66 A.D. His body was decapitated and buried there and a modest monument later erected. Many years later, the Emperor Constantine, in tribute to St. Peter, constructed a large church, so situated on the Vatican hill that the main altar of the church was directly over Peter's tomb. Constantine's church remained for over a thousand years until it was replaced in the sixteenth century by the famous basilica which now dominates the skyline of Rome.

In 1939 workmen engaged in digging a final resting place for the sarcophagus of Pius XI in the grotto of St. Peter's Basilica accidently discovered a subterranean structure. This led to a series of extensive excavations which have been carried on very skillfully over a period of many years beneath the great St. Peter's Church, resulting in priceless archaeological discoveries which have done much to clarify and make more certain the old traditions. For instance, there has been uncovered the old Roman cemetery dating back at least to the first century after Christ with many of its pagan and Christian mausoleums still intact. The foundations of the original Church of Constantine the Great have also been discovered. The axis of that church is also the axis of the much larger church which has replaced it. At the focal point of this axis there was discovered a marble-encased, altar-like monument. Beneath this monument were indications of a grave, and in the grave-like space bones. This monument is directly below the main altar of St. Peter's, the site traditionally assigned to the tomb of St. Peter. (*"The Amazing Search For The Bones of St. Peter,"* Glenn D. Kittler, *The American Weekly,* New York, May 5, 1957; *"Saints Peter and Paul,"* Francis X. Murphy, C.SS.R., *American Ecclesiastical Review,* Washington, January, 1959.)

Church safeguarded from error. If the Church is to be permanent and to continue to teach the true Gospel of Christ until the end of time, she must be divinely protected from doctrinal error. This is what we mean by infallibility, and it is a corollary of the imperishable nature of Christ's Church. Certainly nothing could more effectively bring about the downfall and destruction of the Church than differences and divisions arising over what Christ actually taught. We conclude that Christ's Church cannot err when teaching authoritatively on matters of faith and morals; otherwise Christ's promise, that the gates of hell would not prevail against the Church and that He would be with His Church all days even to the end of the world, would be meaningless.

Church Endowed with Visible Marks

Man's need for the true Church. In the revelation of the Gospels it is apparent that Christ founded a Church to which He wills that all men belong. We have previously demonstrated that man is obligated to honor and worship God, but to do this successfully in a way pleasing to God man needs help. The coming of Christ into the world and the founding of His Church are the answers to man's needs. Man needs the Church which Christ founded and man has an obligation to belong to that Church.

However, there are many churches calling themselves Christian. They differ substantially in their teachings and their manner of worship. Sometimes one church teaches doctrines which are directly opposed to the teachings of another. They cannot all be right. But one of these churches must still be the Church which Christ founded upon His apostles. Because it is of such great importance for men to be able to identify that Church, God must have given to His Church certain characteristics which serve to identify it clearly and set it apart from other so-called Christian churches.

The identifying marks. Christ's Church can be identified because He founded a visible Church which He promised would last until the end of time. Therefore, somewhere in the world it must exist today. It can be identified by certain characteristics or marks which are clearly indicated in the Gospels. Thus the Church which Christ founded must have essential unity, it must be *one* in government, in faith, and in worship; it must be *universal* or Catholic; it must be *apostolic,* i.e., founded on the apostles; it must be *holy* in its teachings and members; and finally, Christ's Church must be *infallible,* insofar as this may be necessary to insure the integrity of doctrinal and moral teachings.

UNITY. Christ intended that His Church should have unity. In His discourse to the apostles at the Last Supper He stressed this need for unity and used the symbolism of the vine and its branches to make it clear to them.

"Abide in me and I in you. As the branch cannot bear fruit of itself unless it remain on the vine, so neither can you unless you abide in me. I am the vine, you are the branches. He who abides in me, and I in him, he bears much fruit; for without me you can do nothing. If anyone does not abide in me, he shall be cast outside as the branch and wither; and they shall gather them up and cast them into the fire, and they shall burn" (John 15:4–6).

At the close of this same discourse to His apostles Christ uttered this prayer for unity. *"Yet not for these only do I pray, but for those also who through their word are to believe in me, that all may be one, even as thou, Father, in me and I in thee; that they also may be one in us, that the world may believe that thou hast sent me" (John 17:20–21).*

These gospel quotations indicate quite clearly that Christ intended that *unity* should be an essential mark of His Church. From other evidence in the Gospels we learn just how this *unity* is to be expressed. It is to be a complete unity, a unity which would exclude all division, otherwise it could not be compared to the perfect unity of the Father and His divine Son. It is apparent that this means that Christ's Church should be one in government, one in doctrine, and one in worship.

One in government. Christ always spoke of His Church, never of His *churches: "upon this rock I will build My Church" (Matthew 16:18).* He compared His Church to a sheepfold, to a kingdom and to a city. *"And other sheep I have that are not of this fold. Them also I must bring, and they shall hear my voice, and there shall be one fold and one shepherd"* *(John 10:16).* *"Every kingdom divided against itself is brought to desolation and every city or house divided against itself will not stand"* *(Matthew 12:25).* All of these analogies imply unity of government or administration. Therefore no division in government can be expected in His Church. The apostles themselves regarded the Church as a single organization under their collective authority. This was evident at the Council of Jerusalem, when they issued a decree binding on all men who had been converted by any of the apostles. These and other facts of history show that there was unity in the government of the Church from the beginning.

One in faith. Christ's commission to His apostles was very simple and very direct: *"Make disciples of all nations . . . teaching them to observe all that I have commanded you."* Almost as if to enforce this direction and to give assurance that it would be carried out Christ added, *"And behold, I am with you all days, even unto the consummation of the world"* *(Matthew 28:19–20).* Of the three types of unity, unity of faith is the most important, because if one believes in Christ and His teachings he will necessarily give obedience to the lawfully constituted authority in the Church and accept the prescribed form of worship.

One in worship. Unity in worship is a practical manifestation of unity in faith. Since the members of Christ's Church are one in faith they will be one also in worship, because unity in faith excludes the possibility of disagreement as to the manner in which God is to be adored and as to the means of sanctification which are to be employed.

CATHOLICITY OR UNIVERSALITY. Christ commanded His apostles to preach the Gospel to *"all nations (Matthew 28:19)* and to *"every creature"* *(Mark 16:15).* They were not to confine their teaching to the men of any particular race or social class. In view of this clear command of Christ we have reason to expect that His Church today is possessed of a membership which in kind and extent can be described as *catholic* or *universal* both socially and numerically.

Socially the membership of the Church should be catholic in the sense that it includes men of every condition and degree of culture, poor and rich, lettered and unlettered. Numerically, the membership of the Church should be widely diffused throughout the world.

Apostolicity. In issuing instructions for the foundation and spread of His Church, Christ spoke to Peter and the apostles as if they were to live always. He promised that He would build His Church on Peter and that the gates of hell would not prevail against it. He commanded them to preach the Gospel to every creature, to make converts of all nations, and promised that He would be with them always until the end of time. Since the apostles themselves were not to live always, they must live in their successors. This is what we mean by apostolicity: The rulers of the Church must derive their authority in lawful succession from the apostles. From the *Acts of the Apostles* and the *Epistles* it is clear that the apostles elected others to assist them in their work, and contemporary writings show that they made definite provisions for their succession. Christ's Church today must be able to trace back its lineage to the apostles.

Holiness. Christ, the Son of God, is Himself the Founder of the Church, the Author of her organization and all her work. Therefore the Church which is certainly holy in her Founder, must be holy in her doctrine, in her worship, and in her object.

Holy in doctrine. Many of those who do not believe in Christ as a divine Person admire nevertheless His moral teachings. For Christ rose far above the level of natural ethics and the practice of the natural virtues, such as truthfulness and honesty. He urged His followers to strive for higher things, to attain the ideals of heroic virtue. He taught deep reverence for God and childlike obedience to Him which should show forth in love of neighbor, humility, meekness, and self-denial, as exemplified in His celebrated *Sermon on the Mount* (Matthew: 5, 6, 7). He summed up all these ideals in one, *"You therefore are to be perfect, even as your heavenly Father is perfect" (Matthew 5:48)*. This doctrine of holiness Christ committed to the Church along with His other teachings, *"teaching them to observe all that I have commanded you" (Matthew 28:20)*.

Holy in members. The Church of Christ as a whole must give evidence at all times that those who faithfully follow her teachings do lead lives of holiness. This is the object of the Church's existence. She must exhibit many instances of the realization of her highest ideals in examples of heroic sanctity among her followers in all ages. This does not mean that all members of Christ's Church will be holy. Man may always abuse the liberty that God has given him and do evil rather than good. Even among the apostles who had lived in intimate association with Christ there was a traitor. We can hardly expect to find a more perfect record amongst the rank and file of Christ's Church. In fact Christ predicted this in some of His parables, in which He likens His kingdom (Church) to a net cast into the sea that gathered in both good and bad fish (Matthew 13:47–50) or to a field where an enemy sowed weeds among the wheat (Matthew 13: 24–30).

INFALLIBILITY. Infallibility means that Christ's Church cannot err when officially teaching and interpreting the truths which Christ delivered to her keeping. This characteristic can be considered as a corollary to the unity of faith required as a characteristic mark of Christ's Church. It is not reasonable to suppose that Christ would teach the true revelation for only three years to a mere handful of people of one generation in a small corner of the world without making provision for the same revelation to be made known, free from error, to the men of every generation until the end of time. If His Church must at all times teach and believe the same body of divine truths, Christ must have empowered His Church to declare with an infallible voice whether a doctrine has been revealed or not, and to expel from her fold all who reject her decision.

If it be admitted that Christ's Church can err in exacting the assent of faith for her teachings then it would follow that there could be no certainty that any particular teaching is actually the teaching of Christ. Hence men could be bound by God under pain of damnation to believe what is false. *"He who does not believe shall be condemned" (Mark 16:16).*

But Christ promised to preserve His Church from error. *"I am with you all days, even to the consummation of the world" (Matthew 28:20),* and, *"I will build my Church, and the gates of hell shall not prevail against it" (Matthew 16:18).* Again, *"The Holy Spirit, whom the Father will send in my name . . . will teach you all things, and bring to your mind whatever I have said to you" (John 14:26).* It is evident therefore, that Christ's Church must claim and exercise the prerogative of infallibility wherever it is possible for widespread doctrinal or moral error to creep into the Church.

REVIEW QUESTIONS

1 Why does the nature of Christ's mission lead one to expect that He must have left behind Him someone to carry on His work?
2 What provision did Christ make for carrying on the work of redemption?
3 What are the essential requisites for a visible society?
4 Why is the visible society which Christ founded called a Church?
5 How do we know that Christ intended to found a visible society?
6 What evidence is there that Christ deliberately gathered followers?
7 What evidence is there that Christ proposed a common goal for His followers?
8 What common means did Christ propose to achieve this goal?
9 What evidence is there that Christ set up a common authority?
10 How do we know that Simon Peter was made head of Christ's Church?
11 What evidence is there that St. Peter acted as head of the Church?
12 What evidence is there that St. Peter was recognized as head of the Church?

13 Why must permanency be a characteristic of Christ's Church?
14 Why is the Bishop of Rome recognized as the successor of St. Peter?
15 Why must the Church be safeguarded from error?
16 In actual practice, how is Christ's Church safeguarded from error?
17 Why do we say that Christ's Church must have characteristic marks by which it may be identified?
18 What are the identifying marks of the Church?
19 Why must the Church possess unity as one of her characteristics and of what does this consist?
20 What is meant by catholicity? Why must the Church possess this as one of her distinguishing marks?
21 What is meant by apostolicity and why must the Church possess this as one of her distinguishing characteristics?
22 What is meant by holiness and why must this be one of the distinguishing marks of the Church?
23 What is infallibility and why must Christ's Church possess infallibility?
24 Why is infallibility necessary for unity in faith?

SUGGESTIONS FOR READING

"The Pope," *Things Catholics Are Asked About,* Martin J. Scott, S.J. New York: P. J. Kenedy & Sons, 1927, Chapter XIII, pp. 82–92. (An explanation of the papacy and why there have been changes in outward circumstances since the time of the first pope, St. Peter.)

"Why Don't Catholics Think for Themselves?" Martin Scott, S.J. *Ibid.,* Chapter VI, pp. 41–46. (There is no betrayal of reason in faithfully following the teachings of Christ's Church.)

Carrier of the Keys, Richard Ginder. Catholic Information Society, 214 West 31st Street, New York 1, N.Y. 15 pp., 5¢. (The pope, the Bishop of Rome, is the successor of St. Peter as head of the Church.)

Thou art the Rock, Richard Ginder. Catholic Information Society. 14 pp., 5¢. (Christ founded His Church on St. Peter.)

Peter: Prince of the Apostles, John B. Harney, C.S.P. The Paulist Press, 401 West 59th Street, New York 19, N.Y., 1948. 32 pp., 10¢ (Proof that Christ gave St. Peter a primacy of honor and jurisdiction. Peter acted as head of the Church.)

United Press International photo

No one seriously disputes that *Pope John XXIII* is the lineal descendant of St. Peter. He "sits in the chair of Peter," and when he officiates at the high altar of St. Peter's Basilica, he stands above the original tomb of St. Peter.

Chapter 13

Identifying Christ's Church

Applying the Tests

SINCE THE CHURCH FOUNDED by Christ has a visible organization and is to last for all time, it must still exist in the world at the present day. Christ's Church can be identified by its distinguishing marks, namely, that it is one, catholic, apostolic, holy, and infallible.

It should be emphasized that these distinguishing marks have been discovered after calm reasoning about the historical evidence found in the Gospels, which reveals the actual intentions, words and acts of Christ in founding His Church. These marks have been determined objectively. They were not subjectively fashioned to fit a particular Church. On the basis of the evidence available it does not seem that any of these marks can be subtracted from the list or new ones added. They must, therefore, stand.

Once the distinguishing marks have been understood and agreed upon, the actual task of appraising the various religious groups which profess to be members of Christ's Church is not difficult. These different religious groups fall readily into three divisions, namely, Protestants, schismatic Greeks and Catholics.

The Protestant Church cannot be the true Church because it is obviously not one in faith or worship or government. Take, for example, the single matter of worship. For Catholics it is the Mass that matters; for them the Holy Sacrifice of the Mass is the central act of Christian worship. Among Protestants there is no unity whatever in worship. At one extreme, High Church Anglicans celebrate "Holy Mass," which in all externals is hardly distinguishable from the Catholic Mass. (Since Anglican orders are not valid, there can be no real Mass.) At the other extreme, some Protestants look upon the Mass as a form of idolatry or superstition. Worship for them will consist of Bible reading, preaching, prayer and song. Ranging between these two extremes there are almost as many variations in worship as there are Protestant denominations. Certainly there is no unity of worship in Protestantism. The same absence of unity is evident as well in faith and in government. Protestantism is divided into a great number of sects professing every shade of opinion. Not one of these sects claims infallibility.

The schismatic Greek Church is not the true Church because it is broken up into a number of divisions, each under an independent authority. It is confined chiefly to Greek and Slavic peoples, and hence cannot claim to be catholic or universal. It does not claim infallibility.

The Catholic Church. Because it is so evident that the Protestant and schismatic Greek Churches lack at least two of the distinguishing marks of Christ's true Church, we need not take time to consider them further. Instead we will examine at greater length the claim of the Catholic Church to be the true Church of Christ, since she seems to have all the necessary identifying marks. If the Catholic Church actually meets the test, this will confirm the judgment that none of the Protestant or schismatic Greek Churches can claim to be the true Church.

The Catholic Church—Christ's Church

We have already examined the characteristics of the Church which Christ founded as these are recorded in the Gospels. Even a very superficial consideration of the Protestant and schismatic Greek Churches was sufficient to show that these divided churches lack at least two or more of the marks characteristic of Christ's Church. We now appeal to our own observations to show that the Catholic Church alone possesses all the characteristics or marks to identify her as being truly Christ's Church.

One in government, faith and worship. The Catholic Church is *one in government* because the people are subject in religious matters to the priests of their parish, the priests and people to the bishop of the diocese, and all are subject to the pope, the center of authority and the bond of apostolic unity. The pope commands the affection and loyalty of all the members of the Church because of his exalted position as head of the Church, the successor of St. Peter, and the Vicar of Christ on earth. The experience of two world wars has proven that allegiance to the pope has not been impaired even when Catholic peoples were found on opposing sides in a devastating war. The Catholic Church is *one in faith* because all her members, whether they be from the most cultured nations or from the most backward peoples, hear the same doctrines from her priests and missionaries and profess the same faith.

The Church teaches what is hard to believe, such profound mysteries as the Trinity, the Incarnation, and the Holy Eucharist. She prescribes many things hard to practice, like personal purity, forgiveness of enemies and the observance of marriage laws which forbid divorce and contraception. At the same time, rejecting all compromise in faith and morals, she nevertheless holds her vast following in willing obedience—a miracle of unity. The Catholic Church is also *one in worship*. Sacrifice has always been considered an essential form of divine worship. So it was among the Jews who offered various libations and burnt offerings to God until the temple of Jerusalem was destroyed soon after the death of Christ. The prophet Malachias predicted very clearly that the sacrifices of the Old Law would be replaced by a new sacrifice, a clean oblation which would be offered up in every part of the world from the rising of the sun until its going down (Malachias 1:10–11). It is most significant that outside of the Catholic Church, with the exception of the Eastern Orthodox Churches, no non-Catholic religion, Protestant or Jewish, today lays claim to any form of sacrificial worship. Only in the Catholic Church is the prophecy of Malachias being literally fulfilled. Moreover, everywhere in the Catholic Church her sacrifice and sacraments are, in essentials, the same, and everywhere the faithful have access to the same ministrations. Such unchanging and unified worship is a phenomenon for which no human or natural explanation can be readily found. The Catholic Church therefore has the triple unity in government, faith, and worship which has been indicated as characteristic of Christ's Church.

Catholic or universal. The Catholic Church is not confined to any single people. She belongs not to any nation or group of nations, but to the world. She counts among her members men of every nation and every race; men who differ in culture, in language, in customs; men in every condition and state of life, the rich and the poor, the learned and the illiterate, men in the humblest walks of life as well as statesmen, scientists, doctors, lawyers, writers. Her followers number about five hundred million—far in excess of the members of any other Christian denomination. Moreover the Catholic Church is not content to rest on her gains. She is still endeavoring to fulfill the command of Christ to teach all nations. The Catholic Church, therefore, has geographical, social, numerical and psychological universality. Even her name, *Catholic*, signifies in effect, "The Teach-ye-all-nations Church."

Apostolic. Christ placed His Church under the government of St. Peter assisted by the apostles: *"I will give to thee the keys of the kingdom of heaven" (Matthew 16:19).* The Catholic Church today is under the government of the lawful successors of St. Peter and the apostles. This is what we mean by apostolic: The Church and the rulers of the Church must be able to trace their authority directly to the apostles. The Catholic Church is the only church which claims that she is ruled by the successor of St. Peter—no one disputes the Catholic Church when she claims that the reigning pope has succeeded to the office of St. Peter. The Catholic Church also points out that the pope is the foundation rock of the Church; that he, like St. Peter, holds the keys of the kingdom of heaven; that as the Shepherd of the whole flock of Christ, the other bishops of the Church are subordinate to him as the other apostles were to St. Peter. The Catholic Church has abundant evidence of her apostolicity. No attempt to discredit this evidence has ever succeeded.

Holy. The Catholic Church teaches, without ceasing, the doctrines of Christ, which are indeed holy. Among the doctrines of Christ she teaches His *counsels of perfection,* whereby men and women voluntarily consecrate themselves to God and bind themselves to His service by vows of poverty, chastity and obedience. Thus there are within the fold of the Church the great religious orders, or societies, of men and women who devote their lives to such practical works of charity as preaching the Gospel in pagan lands, educating youth, relieving the poor, supporting orphans, caring for the sick and the aged, and kindred activities; or who follow the vocation of the contemplative life, spending their days in prayer and mortification.

The holiness of the Church is also manifested in the heroic sanctity of great numbers of her members, many of whom have been raised to her altars by the rigorous process of canonization. Many of these saints are known to those outside the Church as geniuses in the spiritual realm, and are honored by them almost as much as by ourselves. Rightly has the Catholic Church been called the "mother of saints and martyrs."

The Church is also the Church for sinners, for Christ came to redeem man and *"to save what was lost" (Matthew 18:11).* The presence of sinners in the Church of Christ is not an argument against the holiness of the Church: Christ wishes sinners to be saved also. Sinners can find in the Church the forgiveness of sins and the grace to lead holy lives if they will do so. But God has given them free will, and He will not save them in spite of themselves.

Infallible. The Catholic Church alone of all the Christian churches claims and exercises the prerogative of infallibility. By virtue of the promise of Christ that the gates of hell would not prevail against His Church and that He would be with her until the end of time, the Catholic Church claims infallibility whenever and wherever it is possible for widespread error to endanger the Church. We have seen that this is a corollary to the unity of faith which Christ's Church must possess.

The Church is infallible only in matters pertaining to faith and morals because these have a direct bearing on the salvation of souls. Hence the Church does not attempt to give an authoritative judgment on questions of science, mathematics, economics, or the like, when these have no connection whatever with religion.

Infallibility is a protection for the purity of Christ's teaching in the Church. Wherever it would be possible for widespread error to enter the Church, infallibility must be present. The following situations require the protection of infallibility:

1. The decrees of General Councils, when approved and confirmed by the pope. A general (ecumenical) council represents the entire world and its decrees on faith and morals when approved by the pope are binding on all members of the Church. Clearly, then, without the protection of infallibility widespread error could creep into the Church and the promise of Christ would be nullified. Only twenty of these councils have been held during the life of the Church.

2. The *unanimous* teaching of bishops and priests scattered throughout the world. Here again, if all of them believed or taught something false it would be evident that widespread error had crept into the Church and that Christ had failed to keep His promise.

3. For a similar reason, infallibility must safeguard the unanimous belief of all the faithful of the Church scattered throughout the world.

4. The decrees of the pope, when he evidently intends to exercise his supreme teaching authority in matters of faith and morals, must be protected by infallibility. Otherwise, widespread error would creep into the Church, since these decrees will be binding on the whole Church. This is known as papal infallibility. It is the only type of infallibility of which most people are aware. It is quite commonly misunderstood outside the Church. It will be considered here more in detail.

Papal infallibility. The pope is infallible when he speaks *ex cathedra,* that is, when in virtue of his supreme apostolic authority and his position as head of the Church and teacher of all Christians, he defines a doctrine concerning faith or morals to be held by the universal Church. Such a doctrine must belong to the *deposit of faith,* that is, it must be found in Scripture or tradition or both.

The scriptural justification for the Church's claim for papal infallibility is to be found in the texts already quoted, viz., "*I will be with you all days*" etc. (*Matthew 28:20*); "*the gates of hell shall not prevail*" etc. (*Matthew 16:18*); "*Feed my lambs, feed my sheep*" (*John 21:15–17*). On another occasion Christ said to St. Peter: *"Simon, Simon, behold, Satan has desired to have you, that he may sift you as wheat. But I have prayed for thee, that thy faith may not fail; and do thou, when once thou hast turned again, strengthen thy brethren" (Luke 22:31–32).* From this text it is clear that St. Peter was made infallible and that he was to use this gift of infallibility to protect the faith of his brethren. With the death of St. Peter, his office, his prerogatives, his duties, passed on to his successors. The need for papal infallibility is as great in the world today as ever because the enemy of truth will assail the Church as long as it exists.

Even if there were not these clear scriptural passages to prove papal infallibility, there are strong demands from reason that there should be present in the Church an organ of infallibility capable of dealing with corruptions in doctrine and morals whenever they appear. Such an organ of infallibility is found in the pope. His definite decisions spare the Church a multitude of evils.

It should be noted that papal infallibility does not imply personal sinlessness. The pope is infallible only when officially teaching on faith or morals, but he is not impeccable in conduct. He must work out his salvation "in fear and trembling" as the rest of men. He must beware *lest perhaps after preaching to others I myself should be rejected (I Corinthians 9:27).* Neither does papal infallibility imply a power to make new revelations, that is, to disclose to man divine truths previously unknown. The whole of Christian revelation was delivered to the apostles. The pope, in the exercise of infallibility, merely explains a doctrine; he does not add anything to it. Nor are the pope's infallible utterances inspired. God is the author of inspired utterances. He is not the author of papal definitions, but he guarantees them against error.

Membership in Christ's Church

Christ who is God founded a visible society, His Church, which He promised would last to the end of time. Therefore that Church exists in the world today, endowed with certain marks by which men can always identify it. These marks are *unity, catholicity, apostolicity, holiness,* and *infallibility.* No church can be Christ's Church unless it possesses *all* these marks. The Catholic Church alone possesses them: therefore the Catholic Church is the one and only true Church of Christ to which we are obliged to belong if we wish to work out our eternal salvation.

The obligation of membership. Christ's command to preach the Gospel to "every creature" implies a corresponding obligation on all to hear the teachings of the Gospel and to obey them. *"He who does not believe shall be condemned" (Mark 16:16).* Christ gave the apostles and their successors authority to speak in His name: *"As the Father has sent me, I also send you" (John 20:21). "He who hears you, hears me; and he who rejects you, rejects me; and he who rejects me, rejects him who sent me" (Luke 10:16).* No one, therefore, who comes to know and believe the true Church and refuses to join it can be saved. Likewise no one who has known the true Church and forsakes it by heresy or schism can be saved.

Status of those outside the Church. The important truth as to the obligation of membership in Christ's Church is frequently stated in a negative way: "outside the Church there is no salvation." This saying which applies to Christ's true Church, the Catholic Church, sometimes occasions confusion and misunderstanding. It needs to be interpreted properly.

Christ founded His Church as the ordinary means of salvation for all mankind. Furthermore, He placed upon all the obligation of seeking membership in that Church. Hence, anyone who recognizes the Catholic Church as the true Church of Christ and deliberately remains outside that Church cannot be saved.

Membership in the Church implies more than an acceptance of the conclusions of apologetics. It means the ability to make an act of divine faith. Many non-Catholics accept readily enough the conclusions which we reach in apologetics. They are convinced that the Catholic Church is Christ's Church. However, they do not rise to the level of divine faith because they do not possess the proper dispositions which are essential for an act of divine faith. It may be that they do not welcome the truth, and view it with indifference, dislike or hostility. Or it may be that they are not prepared to receive it with the proper gratitude, piety and submissiveness. Or it may be that with the proper dispositions they still humbly await, in God's own good time, the gift which makes possible an act of divine faith. Be that as it may, God alone can judge the responsibility of the individual who, although reasonably convinced, delays outside the fold of the Catholic Church.

Moreover, God condemns no one except for a deliberate and grave fault. Those who through inculpable ignorance are either not aware of Christ's command to be members of His Church or do not recognize the Catholic Church as His true Church, will not be condemned on that account. If such persons serve God faithfully according to their conscience and have a sincere desire to do His will, they can be said to have, implicitly, the desire to become members of Christ's Church. One who in good faith is thus outside the membership of the visible Church is sometimes said to belong to the Church by implicit desire.

Therefore, a baptized Protestant who has lived all his life as a Protestant without ever having a serious doubt that he is in the true Church will be saved if he dies in the state of grace. The fact that he is not a Catholic will not be held against him. On the other hand, no Catholic will be saved if he has the misfortune to die outside the state of grace. The fact that he is a Catholic will not save him under such circumstances. Then there are non-baptized persons who may never have heard even the name of Christ. Such as these are clearly "outside the Church." Is there no chance of salvation for them? All that we can say is this: God wills that all be saved, He will not deny grace to him who does his best. To one who is faithful to the natural law God will give sufficient light and help to do whatever else is necessary for salvation.

These interpretations do not render meaningless the statement, "outside the Church there is no salvation." Certainly there is no salvation for one who recognizes the Catholic Church to be truly Christ's Church and knowingly and willingly remains outside. Neither can we say that there is salvation for one who has serious doubts about his church being Christ's Church, but makes no effort to find the true Church.

Also we have no doubt that salvation is not easy for those who do not belong to the visible membership of the Catholic Church. They are deprived of the abundant graces which are available to those who have the help of the seven sacraments and the Holy Sacrifice of the Mass as their form of worship. Catholics, favored as they are, have an obligation, at least in charity, to do what they can to make the Faith available to those now outside Christ's Church.

REVIEW QUESTIONS

1. How were the identifying marks for Christ's Church established?
2. Why is it possible to eliminate rather quickly all of the Protestant churches as serious contenders for consideration as Christ's true Church?
3. Why is the schismatic Greek Church (or Eastern Orthodox) readily eliminated from consideration as Christ's true Church?
4. Is there evidence that the Catholic Church has unity in government? Explain briefly.
5. Is there evidence that the Catholic Church is one in faith? Explain briefly.
6. Is there evidence that the Catholic Church is one in worship? Explain briefly.
7. Is there evidence for the universality of the Catholic Church? Explain briefly.
8. Is there evidence for the apostolicity of the Catholic Church? Explain briefly.
9. Is there evidence for the holiness of the Catholic Church? Explain briefly.

10 Is there evidence that the Catholic Church claims and exercises the prerogative of infallibility? Explain briefly.

11 What is understood by papal infallibility and why is it necessary?

12 Why is it said that everyone has an obligation to seek membership in the Catholic Church?

13 What is the meaning and scope of the teaching: "Outside the Church there is no salvation"?

14 What is the status of one who cannot in good conscience accept the Catholic Church?

15 What is the status of one who sees the reasonableness of the claims of the Catholic Church but feels positively repelled by Catholicism?

16 What is the status of one who doubts very much the truth of his religious denomination, but feels that it is too late for him to make a change?

17 Under what conditions can a non-Catholic find salvation in his Protestant church?

18 What does membership in the Catholic Church imply?

SUGGESTIONS FOR READING

"Anti-Catholic Prejudice," *Things Catholics Are Asked About,* Martin J. Scott, S. J. New York: P. J. Kenedy & Sons, 1927, Chapter XV, pp. 100–107. (An analysis of some of the reasons for this prejudice.)

"Are Catholics Credulous?" *Ibid.,* Chapter X, pp. 62–67. (Catholics, as a body, are far from being credulous, superstitious or fanatical.)

"Does It Matter What We Believe?" *Ibid.,* Chapter VIII, pp. 51–57.

"Is One Religion as Good as Another?" *Ibid.,* Chapter VII, pp. 46–51.

"Papal Infallibility," *Ibid.,* Chapter XIV, pp. 92–100.

"Salvation Outside the Church," *Ibid.,* Chapter IX, pp. 57–62. (An explanation of the scriptural passage: *"He that believeth and is baptized shall be saved: but he that believeth not shall be condemned" [Mark 16:16].*)

"Difficulties Surmounted—Papal Infallibility," *Rebuilding a Lost Faith,* John L. Stoddard. New York: P. J. Kenedy & Sons, 1924, Chapter XIV, pp. 145–154.

In Search of Truth, Richard Ginder. Catholic Information Society, 214 West 31st Street, New York 1, N.Y. 14 pp., 5¢. (Seventy-five million Americans without any religious affiliation, 256 different Christian denominations—how does one find the Church established by Christ?)

It Does Make A Difference! Richard Ginder. Catholic Information Society. 16 pp., 5¢. (One is obliged to belong to Christ's Church which was founded on St. Peter and the apostles and which is presided over today by the Bishop of Rome.)

Looking for Religious Truth? Richard Ginder. Catholic Information Society. 15 pp., 5¢. (Look for the Church which teaches with the authority of Christ.)

The Popes—Infallible Teachers, John B. Harney, C.S.P. The Paulist Press, 401 West 59th Street, New York 19, N.Y., 1948. 32 pp., 10¢. (The unity which Christ willed for His Church and His promise to be with the Church for all time would mean nothing without the infallibility of the successors of St. Peter. This infallibility is explained and proved.)

The Catholic Church and the Bible, Wilfred G. Hurley, C.S.P. The Paulist Press, 1934. 24 pp., 10¢. (Proves that the Bible alone is not a sufficient rule of faith or guide to the teachings of Christ. The Catholic Church is Christ's Church.)

The Catholic Church is the Church of Christ, Wilfred G. Hurley, C.S.P. The Paulist Press, 1934. 23 pp., 10¢. (It meets all the tests for the "marks" of Christ's Church.)

One Church Is Not as Good as Another! Wilfred G. Hurley, C.S.P. The Paulist Press, 1934. 10¢. (Explains indifferentism, shows its fallacy and danger. Shows the necessity of following Christ's commands.)

The Pope Is Infallible! Wilfred G. Hurley, C.S.P. The Paulist Press, 1934, 24 pp., 10¢.

Father L. Rumble, a convert from Anglicanism, has written a series of pamphlets on Protestant denominations. Listed here are five of these pamphlets which deal with the five denominations numerically strongest in the United States. Each account is factually and moderately written.

The Baptists, L. Rumble, M.S.C. Radio Replies Press Society, St. Paul 1, Minnesota. 35 pp. 15¢.

The Episcopalians. 32 pp. 15¢.

The Lutherans. 44 pp. 15¢.

The Methodists. 36 pp. 15¢.

The Presbyterians. 34 pp. 15¢.

Are Only Catholics Saved? 24 pp. 15¢. (Fifty-seven questions and answers dealing frankly with every aspect of the proposition: "Outside the Catholic Church there is no salvation.")

Wide World photo

A partial view of an immense throng in front of St. Peter's Basilica. St. Peter's and the Vatican are daily witnesses of the unity, the holiness, the universality, and the apostolicity of the Catholic Church.

Chapter 14

The Church, God's work

We have proved that Christ founded a Church and that the Catholic Church is that Church. In doing this we began, so to speak, at the beginning and worked forward to the Church as we find it today. There are some who prefer an easier and shorter approach to this objective. They would start with the Catholic Church as we find it today, a living fact, and work back to its divine institution. They would argue that the unique and marvelous characteristics of the Catholic Church cannot be due to any natural cause but can be explained only by the action of some all-powerful, intelligent, supernatural Being whom we call God.

The Church, a Unique Institution

The reasoning runs something like this. The Catholic Church exists today as a unique and remarkable institution. She appeals to all men, whatever their race or country. She attracts young and old, rich and poor, learned and ignorant, civilized and uncivilized, with truths to be believed and a code of morals to be observed that do not come easy to human nature. She is to be found all over the world and, as of this day and age, claims almost one half billion adherents. Down through the ages her influence on every phase of human activity has been tremendous. She is evidently indestructible. No other institution can compare with her.

Survived pagan Rome. If you delve into the history of the Catholic Church, you find that she traces her beginnings back to the time of Christ and the old pagan Roman Empire. Shortly after her birth all the power of Imperial Rome was marshalled to wipe her off the face of the earth. Incredibly savage persecutions were employed, the most bloody and most cruel that human ingenuity could devise, to intimidate her members and to compel them to renounce Christianity. But Christians died by the thousands, willingly embracing martyrdom rather than compromise in any way their allegiance to Christianity. Yes, Christianity lives on in the Catholic Church and pagan Rome is gone! Ironically enough, in the city of Rome itself, Catholic churches and institutions, in many cases, rest on the ruins of pagan temples and, in some instances, have been built with stones from pagan monuments.

Continued existence miraculous. Not only did the Catholic Church survive almost three hundred years of persecutions by pagan Rome, but she witnessed the fall and dissolution of this once mighty empire. However, this was not the end of suffering and persecution for Christ's Church—history bears witness that it was only a beginning. Down through the ages it has continued, first in this country, now in that country. These have been for the most part temporary setbacks, and the Church has continued to progress and to spread. Her continued existence is a standing miracle. She must be God's work!

Lord Macaulay's testimony. There is a famous, oft-quoted passage from the Protestant writer, Lord Macaulay, which has pertinence here:

> There is not and there never was on this earth a work of human policy so well deserving of examination as the Roman Catholic Church. . . . The proudest royal houses are but of yesterday, when compared with the line of the Supreme Pontiffs. . . . The republic of Venice came next in antiquity. But the republic of Venice was modern when compared with the Papacy; and the republic of Venice is gone, and the Papacy remains. The Papacy remains, not in decay, not a mere antique, but full of life and youthful vigor. The Catholic Church is still sending forth to the farthest ends of the world missionaries as zealous as those who landed in Kent with Augustine, and still confronting hostile kings with the same spirit with which she confronted Attila. . . . Nor do we see any sign which indicates that the term of her long dominion is approaching. She saw the commencement of all the ecclesiastical establishments that now exist in the world; and we feel no assurance that she is not destined to see the end of them all. . . . It is not strange that in the year 1799, even sagacious observers should have thought that, at length, the hour of the Church of Rome was come. An infidel power ascendant, the Pope dying in captivity, the most illustrious prelates of France living in a foreign country on Protestant alms, the noblest edifices which the munificence of former ages had consecrated to the worship of God turned into temples of Victory, or into banqueting houses for political societies. . . . But the end was not yet. . . . Anarchy had its day. A new order of things rose out of the confusion, new dynasties, new laws, new titles; and amidst them emerged the ancient religion. . . . Europe was full of young creations, a

French empire, a kingdom of Italy, a Confederation of the Rhine. Nor had the late events affected only territorial limits and political institutions. The distribution of property, the composition and spirit of society, had, through a great part of Catholic Europe, undergone a complete change. But the unchangeable Church was still there (Macaulay, *Essay on Ranke's History of the Popes*).

Survived global conflicts. Lord Macaulay's *Essay* speaks about events that happened near the beginning of the nineteenth century. But history has repeated itself in the twentieth century and will, no doubt, continue to repeat itself. In World Wars I and II (1914–18 and 1939–45) the greater part of the world was at war. The nations of Europe particularly were locked in mortal combat. Catholic nations and peoples were ranged on both sides of the conflict. The pope at Rome, sitting in the precarious seat of neutrality, strove in vain to bring about peace. From a human point of view the Church was in great danger.

The enemies of the Church, especially in World War I, gloated over the impending destruction of the papacy and the universal Catholic Church. No matter who might win the war or what else might happen, they were confident that the power of the papacy and the influence of the Catholic Church were at an end. So sure were they that this would happen that they openly boasted about it in the public press.

But what really happened? When the war was over, the Catholic Church emerged from the wreckage of Europe stronger than before. As a result of the war the map of Europe was remade, kingdoms and dynasties had fallen, boundary lines were radically changed, new nations and new governments arose. Almost alone the Catholic Church survived unchanged. The prophets of doom for the Catholic Church had been confounded.

World War II presented similar and even greater dangers

for the Catholic Church in Europe.The enemies of the Church were again hopeful that this would be the long-awaited death knell for the papacy. But the lesson of World War I was still fresh in their minds so they refrained from public predictions. This time it was even hoped in some quarters that Vatican City would be bombed out of existence. There were many anxious days and nights but the Vatican and the great St. Peter's Basilica, the mother church of Christendom, remained virtually unscathed. Throughout the world the Church suffered great financial losses in damaged buildings of every kind but her moral strength and prestige were greater than ever before.

Survived internal dangers. Thus far we have spoken chiefly of external threats to the life of the Church. But very large organizations are sometimes more vulnerable to internal difficulties than to external pressures. The Catholic Church, a world-wide organization, has certainly had her share of internal difficulties. The late Archbishop Sheehan points out very frankly some of the internal dangers which the Church has confronted in the past.

> The dangers to the Papacy came from within as well as from without. An elective monarchy, notoriously the most unstable of all forms of government, it attracted the ambition of worldly ecclesiastics and, for a time during the Middle Ages, became a prize for which rival monarchs intrigued, each trying to secure it for his own minion. It was, therefore, threatened with the twofold evil of an unworthy occupant and a disappointed faction. Hence, we find, as a fact, that there have been some few Popes, incompetent and even wicked, and that disastrous schisms have occurred from time to time. Any one of these schisms, any one of these Popes, if he had held a secular throne and were equally unfit for his office, would have brought the most powerful dynasty crashing to the ground (Sheehan, *Apologetics and Catholic Doctrine,* p. 16).

Unity miraculous. The Church has indeed survived the dangers of heresy and schism which would have rent "the seamless robe of Christ." But more than this, despite the fierce tugging of these dangers, the pressures of nationalistic pride, and the varying temperaments of peoples and races, the Church has preserved intact unity in government, unity in faith, and unity in worship. This unity, which we have described in greater detail in a previous chapter, is a marvel that is beyond human explanation. In historical retrospect, this threefold unity of the Church is clearly miraculous. Again we must conclude the hand of God is surely here!

The Church Confronting Present Dangers

The carnage and destruction of World War II were scarcely at an end when a new and possibly greater danger for the Church quickly appeared in the resurgence and spread of communism. Although communism in Russia was almost prostrated during the war, it quickly recovered. With the aid of Christian nations (which since have had reason to regret the assistance) the Communist government quickly recouped its losses and emerged from the aftereffects of the war stronger than ever. By sheer might the Communist government of Russia took over the control of weak neighboring nations. Before long the so-called "iron curtain" descended on formerly free peoples, including predominantly Catholic countries like Lithuania, Czechoslovakia and Poland. The Church has, of course, suffered greatly in these countries. But we cannot dwell on this here at any length.

The situation of the Catholic Church in Poland, by all odds the best in the "satellite countries," typifies the struggle between the Church and communism. It was well described by a *New York Times* correspondent shortly after he was expelled from the country for having "probed too deeply" into Polish affairs. "In the life of Poland," this correspondent said, fundamental power belongs to the Soviet Union, but fundamental influence still belongs to the Roman Catholic Church. . . .

It was because of the existence of the Soviet Union—more bluntly, because of the ever-present shadow of the Soviet Army—that communism was able to come to power in Poland and has been maintained in power.

It is because of the existence of the Church—more precisely, because of the intense devotion of the huge majority of Poles to it—that communism has had virtually no impact on the emotions and loyalties of the Polish people.

The two great realities—Catholicism and the Soviet shadow behind Polish communism—act and react on each other constantly. It is largely because of the existence of the Church that the Polish Communists, who know that at best they only share authority with it, have had to strike out on some unexplored Socialist roads to maintain order and even the semblance of control.

And the existence of the Soviet Union puts constant limitations on the actions, decisions, and pronouncements of the Church in Poland. Fear that the overthrow of Polish communism would bring the Soviet Army into the country has made the Church forego the use of its strength against Polish communism. (A. M. Rosenthal, *The New York Times,* December 3, 1959.)

The religious Armageddon is yet to come. The battle lines are clearly drawn—atheistic communism on the one side, Catholicism on the other. However, the battle is more than a struggle between religious and anti-religious forces. It is a life-and-death struggle for the religious, political, and economic freedoms we now enjoy. On the political and economic front it is Russia and her satellites against the United States and the "Western" nations.

What is to be the outcome? We do not know. Unquestionably the Catholic Church faces the greatest challenge of her nineteen–century career. We can have no doubt about the final outcome, but what lies between, we do not know. Clearly, this is no time for weak-kneed Catholics! All must pull together and strive as if everything depended on the human energies in the Church and all must pray as if everything depended, as it does ultimately, on God.

Survival Impossible for a Merely Human Institution

As a merely human institution the Church could never have survived from the time of the apostles to the present day. But she has survived through all the vast social and political changes, the revolutions and catastrophes, and the global wars that have affected the world, and particularly Europe, since the days of the Roman emperors. The Church has survived in spite of persecution and political intrigue; in spite of heresy and schism among her members; in spite of the worldliness, the weakness or the incompetency of some of the popes. Finally, she has survived, not as a mere shadow of her former greatness, but in unimpaired vigor. She has spread to the farthest corners of the globe. She has kept intact her unity in government, in faith, and in worship. Such a survival is nothing, if not miraculous! The Church must, therefore, be the work of God.

REVIEW QUESTIONS

1. Why is the Catholic Church called a unique institution?
2. What is remarkable about the survival of the Church and the demise of pagan Rome?
3. Why is the continued existence of the Church called a "standing miracle"?
4. If the existence of the Church is a standing miracle, what does this imply?
5. Does Macaulay's statement imply belief in the Church as a divinely established institution? Why?
6. What is meant by saying: "The dangers to the papacy came from within as well as from without"?
7. What is meant by saying that the threefold unity of the Church is miraculous?
8. What is the chief danger confronting the Church on a world-wide scale at present?

9 Why is it necessary for all Christians to cooperate in the battle against communism?

10 Why do we say that a merely human institution could not survive from the time of the apostles to the present day?

SUGGESTIONS FOR READING

Recognizing Miracles, Richard Ginder. Catholic Information Society, 214 West 31st Street, New York 1, N.Y. 15 pp. 5¢. (Present-day miracles in the Church, at Lourdes or elsewhere, confirm the claim of the Catholic Church to be the true Church.)

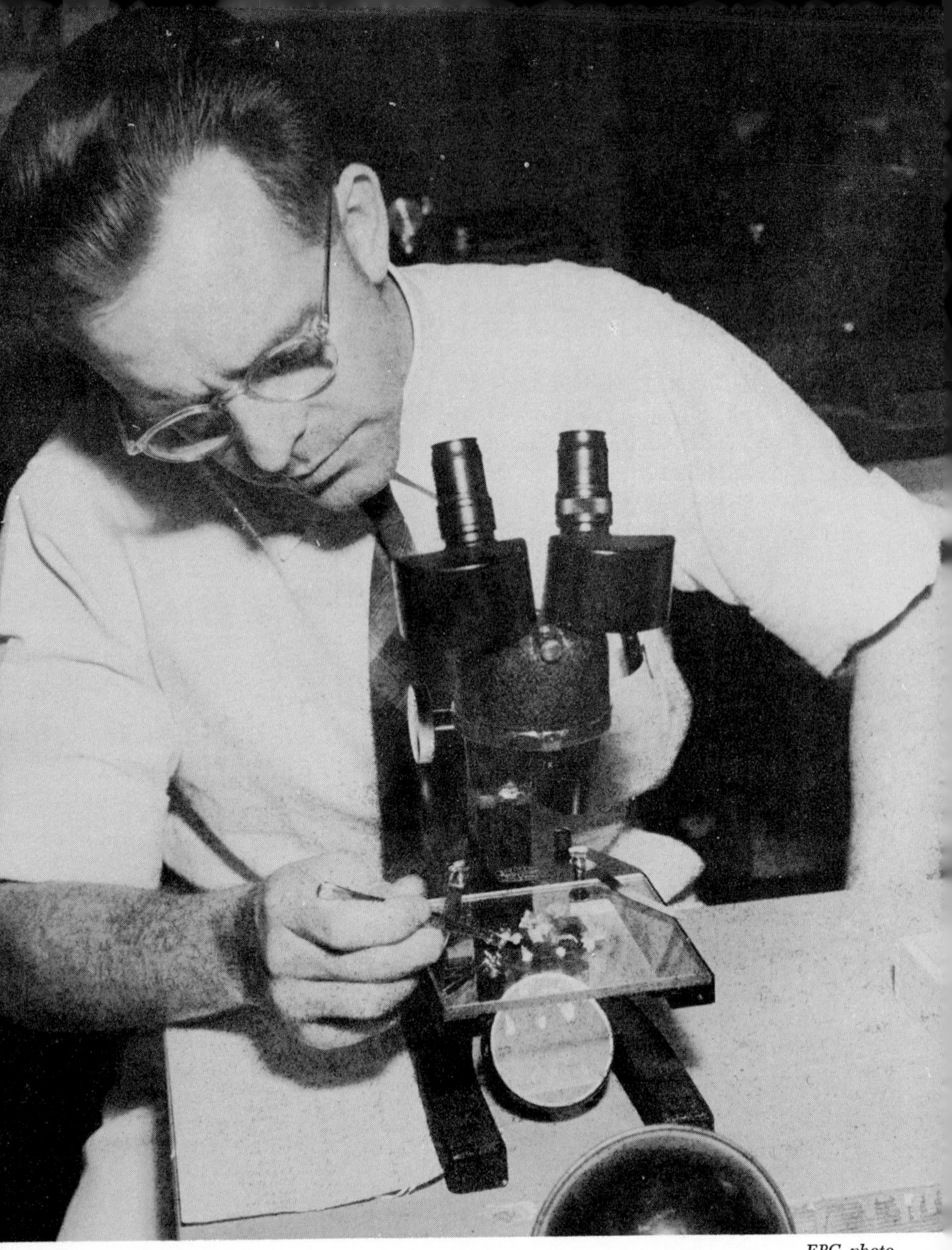

FPG photo

The microscope is a very useful instrument to assist man in his study of many things. It will reveal many kinds of bacteria, but it will not help us to see patriotism, liberty, virtue, or even life itself. It is wholly unreasonable to expect it to discover man's soul or his spiritual faculties of reasoning and free will.

Chapter 15

The Godless

Atheism

We have considered various arguments from reason to prove the existence of God. These arguments are *conclusive* but not *coercive,* that is, they should be convincing to any person who will consider them with an unprejudiced mind. But these arguments will not force one to believe in God. They will not convince a prejudiced or foolish mind, or one who does not want to believe, or one who has no time to think about such matters. There is an old proverb which has an obvious application here: "You can lead a horse to water but you cannot make him drink."

Therefore, despite the fact that all nature proclaims most eloquently the existence of God, there are some who deny, ignore, or doubt His existence. There are various categories and degrees of this unbelief which fall under the general headings of atheism and agnosticism. Those who do not believe in the existence of God are called *atheists* while those who doubt His existence are termed *agnostics*. Both of these terms are derived from the Greek language. *Atheism* comes from two Greek words meaning literally "away from God." *Agnosticism* is derived from two Greek words meaning "one who does not know."

The refutation of atheism in its different forms is to be found essentially in the various arguments from reason which prove the existence of God. These arguments we have already considered in chapters two and three.

There are two general classes of atheists: the *positive* atheist, who openly denies the existence of God, and the *practical* atheist, who has nothing to say about the existence of God but who lives his life as if God did not exist. Among the positive atheists there are three types which we can identify. There is the *militant* atheist, who attempts to support his hostility to the idea of God by some sort of argument. There is the *materialistic* atheist, who attributes to the matter of the universe some strange and unexplained power of bringing itself into existence and thus by implication gets rid of God by making Him unnecessary or impossible. Then there is the *pantheistic* atheist, who virtually denies the existence of God because he equates God with the material universe. He affirms that everything is God, and that all the things we see around us are part of God. In this way he destroys the idea of God by reducing Him to material form. *Positive* atheists, as we have described them, are relatively few today.

The militant atheist abounds wherever communism is entrenched. He seems to be committed to rooting out God from the minds and hearts of men. In all Communist-dominated countries there is a hard core of atheists who make every effort to stamp out all organized religion through propaganda, proscription and outright persecution. Although these Communist leaders have been diabolically clever in their propaganda and fiendish in their persecution, they have not, as yet, been very successful. Even though they have indoctrinated young children in atheism and have tried to instill in them a hatred of God and religion, there is reason to believe that even here they have been far from sucessful. In the effort to stamp out God and religion, Communists are up against both the universal belief of mankind in a Supreme Being and the universal inner need of man to pay honor and reverence to that Supreme Being. In the United States, however, militant atheists in recent years seem to be few and far between. There is an organized group known as the "United Secularists of America," which publishes an atheistic journal. This group is notable chiefly for its nuisance value. It regularly opposes all gestures favorable to God and religion, such as the motto "In God We Trust" on our coinage, the reading of the Bible in schools, chaplains for the Armed Forces and for Congress, and the like.

The materialistic atheist, whose cult is scientism, is likewise not very common today. Many, if not most, of our outstanding scientists are men of strong religious convictions. "A little dabbling in science may lead men's minds away from God, but much dabbling will bring men's minds back to God."

The pantheistic atheist is found chiefly in certain esoteric philosophical and religious groups. Christian Science, founded by Mary Baker Eddy around 1880, is perhaps the best-known example of pantheism in the United States. It seems to appeal to certain well-to-do people, and has good financial backing, but is not numerically important.

The practical atheist. Far more numerous than all types of positive atheists combined, are what we have called *practical* atheists. Without ever thinking much about whether there is or is not a God, these people live as if there were no God. They are secularists with a vengeance. Some of them may have become so engulfed in amoral living as to have an aversion for God and religion. Others may have become so immersed in business or professional pursuits that they have no time for God or religion.

Agnosticism

The agnostic is a professional I-do-not-know man. He claims that it is impossible for the finite human mind to have any knowledge of God. If asked whether or not God exists, he would reply: "I do not know, and there is no way to find out anything with certainty." Since he denies the possibility of being certain about the existence of God, he necessarily refuses to accept anything that may be said about the nature and attributes of God. The agnostic is quick to say that he does not deny that God exists; neither does he affirm that God exists. He is convinced that there is nothing we can know on this subject. In his opinion, if there is a God, He is so incomprehensible and so far above and beyond the human mind that we can neither affirm nor deny anything about Him.

Agnosticism takes it for granted either that we cannot know anything which we do not perceive by means of our senses or that we cannot know anything about the infinite. Neither of these suppositions is true.

It is true that human knowledge does indeed begin with the senses. But once the senses have conveyed their information we constantly use our reason to arrive at a further knowledge of things which are not visible, even though they are material. Radio waves furnish a good example. No one has ever seen, heard, felt or tasted radio waves in themselves, although the air is literally filled with them at all times. They are not only all around and about us, but they actually pass through our bodies. We do not perceive them by any of our senses, but we do experience their effects in the radio programs which are being transmitted day and night. From these effects we reason to the existence of the radio waves. This is by no means an isolated example from the physical world. It happens again and again in a thousand different ways.

Therefore the fact that God is invisible does not of itself make it impossible for us to know that He exists. Neither does the fact that He is infinite, while we are finite, make Him completely unknowable. When we reason about the visible universe we know that a Supreme Being must have created it as we have already demonstrated in the earlier proofs for God's existence. At the same time we learn much about God's nature, such as His attributes of intelligence, wisdom, and power, which are so clearly reflected in His creation. And there are many other things we can learn about God if we will only be observant and use our reason, which is the task we impose upon ourselves in our study of apologetics. Since we can, as a matter of fact, know many things about God, agnosticism is not only unreasonable, but it is also untrue.

The mild agnostic. There is a milder form of agnosticism in which it is not claimed that we can know nothing about God, but that we can know nothing with absolute certainty. The distance between the milder form and out-and-out agnosticism is not very great. Instead of simply claiming that we can know nothing about God, the mild agnostic is more diplomatic. He is willing to concede that what we say about God may possibly be true, or close to the truth or, at least, it is probably leading one in the right direction. But of course we cannot be positively and finally certain that it is true. The mild agnostic is frequently an *indifferentist* in religion; that is, he is indifferent to all religious beliefs. He does not hold to any particular faith nor claim that all others are wrong. Rather, he is of the opinion that there is something of good in all religious beliefs so that it is impossible to say with certainty that any one of them is entirely correct.

Between the agnostic and the atheist there is little practical difference. Agnosticism readily leads to atheism. Although the agnostic does not deny God's existence, his denying that we can know anything about God really amounts to about the same thing. For all practical purposes, agnosticism can rightly be considered a form of atheism.

The atheist or the agnostic, without a firm belief in God, is a lonely man. He is greatly handicapped in life and in death. One who has lost his faith in God and who has experienced the emptiness of atheism would not ordinarily wish to propagate his unbelief or wish to pass it on to his children. For the believer it is difficult to conceive how one could go all through life as a really convinced atheist or agnostic without at least some serious doubts as to the reasonableness of one's unbelief. So strong and undeniable are the evidences for God's existence that some writers say that complete atheism is impossible, that it is not possible for one to be a convinced atheist at all times and under all circumstances throughout one's lifetime. Well-attested experiences during World War II seem to bear out this conviction. Thus there was a well-known saying, "There are no atheists in foxholes," meaning of course that under the stress of battle, facing the possibility of imminent death, men do call upon God for assistance and protection who formerly had never given Him a thought or who doubted or denied His existence.

The Development of an Atheist

Apart from atheism as an ideology or as a creed, as is found in communism, how does one who formerly believed in God fall into the unbelief of agnosticism or atheism? Specifically, how can one explain the case, for instance, of a young man, brought up in a good Catholic home, educated in Catholic schools, who seems suddenly to lose his faith and apparently to give up all belief in God? Before attempting to answer this question let us consider three introductory remarks. First of all one does not *suddenly* lose faith in God, all appearances to the contrary notwithstanding. There is a gradual weakening of faith caused by repeated infidelities which may go on over a considerable period of time before it happens that one no longer has faith.

Secondly, the reasons alleged by one who loses faith are rarely, if ever, the true reasons. Such a one will usually put the blame on someone else: religious people are hypocrites; priests are always talking money, or the like. There are underlying reasons that may not appear on the surface and which the party concerned will not willingly admit even to himself, much less divulge to others. More often than not these reasons become buried deep in one's subconscious mind.

Thirdly, loss of faith is seldom attributable to intellectual difficulties. More often it is a difficulty in the practical order. Among the reasons which serve to explain loss of faith in God, the following appear to the writer as important. They are arranged in the order of their seeming frequency.

Conflict of habit with faith. When one has become immersed in serious habitual sin there is set up a conflict between one's convictions as a believer in God and one's actual life in opposition to these convictions. This state of affairs cannot continue indefinitely. Sooner or later something has to give. Either one gives up the habit of sin or one tries to rationalize himself out of belief in God.

Character immaturity. Young people especially, who may have inferiority complexes, like to say and do things that startle or shock others. Atheism is different. Adopting this as a pose, in the beginning, appeals to their vanity. In their efforts to convince others they succeed only in convincing themselves. Or it may be that pride prompts the desire to be superior to and independent of others. The atheist makes himself independent even of God.

Worship of intellectual ability. Some people worship "brains" to the exclusion of all else. Thus young people especially, who are impressed by cleverness and mental brilliance, may be dazzled by the display of learning and the cocksure cynicism of atheistic companions or teachers who, under the pretense of utmost fairness, can sweep aside cherished beliefs and practices as something unworthy of really intelligent people. This may sorely try the faith of one who is unable to give a reason for his beliefs or to answer the objections of others. Thus the foundations of faith are weakened, and if one is continuously or repeatedly exposed to the danger, faith may be lost entirely.

An act of rebellion. In many instances atheism has developed out of resistance to certain unpleasant experiences associated with religion. Thus a Protestant youth may inwardly rebel against long, dull and tiresome sermons and a religious service that appears to him drab and unpleasant. As a consequence he drops church attendance at the first opportunity and may never return again. In other instances the seeming inconsistencies of most Protestant sects, and the absence of any clear and authoritative voice on religious truths and the consequent conflicting opinions, tend to confuse some young people and lead them to conclude that no teaching of religion can be accepted as certain. In the case of Catholic youth it has happened that overzealous concern of parents for the religious practice of their children produced results quite at variance with what the parents intended. Thus the habit of missing Mass has been traced to constant harping of a parent on attendance at an early Mass, or to the evident and open mistrust of parents that a son or daughter is actually attending Mass. Again imprudent pressure by a parent on a young person to receive Communion with the family, Sunday after Sunday, has led to unworthy Communions, bad confessions and loss or near loss of faith.

REVIEW QUESTIONS

1 What is meant by saying that the arguments for the existence of God are conclusive but not coercive?

2 What is an agnostic and how does he differ from an atheist?
3 What is a positive atheist?
4 What is a practical atheist?
5 What is a militant atheist?
6 What is a materialistic atheist?
7 What is a pantheistic atheist?
8 What is a mild agnostic?
9 What is meant by the phrase: "There are no atheists in foxholes"?
10 What are some reasons for loss of faith?
11 Is loss of faith apt to occur suddenly?
12 What is meant by conflict of habit with faith?
13 What has character immaturity to do with loss of faith?
14 How can worship of intellectual ability contribute to loss of faith?
15 What connection is there between an act of rebellion and loss of faith?

SUGGESTIONS FOR READING

Faith, Lost and Found, James Fenelon Finley, C.S.P. The Paulist Press, 401 West 59th Street, New York 19, N.Y., 1953. 28 pp., 10¢. (This is an allegory which explains what leads to loss of faith and how would-be atheists come into being.)

God's Own Truth, Richard Ginder. Catholic Information Society, 214 West 31st Street, New York 1, N.Y. 16 pp., 5¢. (Atheism solves nothing and is unreasonable.)

Science and Atheism, Ulrich A. Hauber. The Paulist Press, 1945. 32 pp., 10¢. (A commentary and reply to "Science and the Supernatural" by the militant atheist, A. J. Carlson, who is also a well-known physiologist. With the searchlight of calm reasoning it lays bare the contempt, cynicism, and unfairness of the atheist toward God, faith, and religion.)

The Unknown God, John A. O'Brien. The Paulist Press, 1949. 20 pp., 10¢. (Agnosticism and practical atheism in operation; the vagueness and obscurity in the conception of God held by certain philosophers and supposed "leaders" of religious thought.)

FPG photo

A thoughtful student finds no difficulties in the pseudo-objections brought up by those who do not want to believe in God.

Chapter 16

Some pseudo-difficulties

Evolution

THE SUBJECT OF *evolution* enters into an apologetics course only, so to speak, by the back door. Unfortunately, many people consider that evolution, either as a theory or as a fact, disproves the existence of God or dispenses with the necessity of believing in Him. Thus evolution qualifies, although erroneously, as an "objection" to belief in the existence of God. It is for this reason that it receives a mention in apologetics.

There is much very muddled thinking, and consequently

much misunderstanding, about evolution. Like the term freedom of speech, for example, the word *evolution* seems to cover a multitude of things. Any dictionary will give several meanings. The definition closest to our use of the term defines evolution broadly, as the process by which, through a series of changes, any living organism or group of organisms has acquired the characteristics which distinguish it. Thus a flower is the evolution of the bud, an oak tree evolves from an acorn dropped into the ground. We would also include nonliving things because we are concerned with evolution as a natural and orderly process of development and growth following as a result of the creative act of God in calling the universe into being.

Materialistic evolution. We have many theories which seek to explain how all things in the universe came to their present state of development. Nearly all of these theories presuppose, or at least do not deny, the creative act of God. However, as we have already discussed in chapter fifteen, there are atheists who oppose or deny belief in the existence of God. Certainly any theory of evolution proposed or subscribed to by an atheist will seek to leave God completely out of the picture. Otherwise the atheist would no longer be an atheist. All theories of evolution which implicitly or explicitly try to dispense with the existence of God are lumped together under the general heading of "Materialistic Evolution." Materialistic evolution is directly opposed to belief in the existence of God. As it happens, such theories are no longer considered good science or good logic. These theories rest on the shaky premise that things happen by chance, that matter is self-existent and eternal or that matter contains within itself certain mysterious powers that enable it to evolve in marvelous ways. It is far harder to accept theories of materialistic evolution than it is to believe in the existence of a Supreme Being.

Fact, theory, or hypothesis. In proving the existence of God from the evidence of order and design in the universe we have already disproved and disposed of all materialistic theories of evolution. But what about other theories of evolution? Are they in any way opposed to belief in God or do they detract from the recognition due to God? To make our answer clear and convincing let us define our terms and our degrees of certitude.

When man seeks to know the why and wherefore of all that he finds in the universe, he acquires knowledge laboriously and gradually. He may begin his search for an explanation of some phenomenon in nature by making an educated guess which we call a *hypothesis*. As this hypothesis seems to be borne out more and more by observation and experiment it is more carefully formulated and becomes dignified by the title of *theory*.[1] As time goes on and the theory seems to explain satisfactorily and invariably all facets of the phenomenon of nature under investigation, it becomes known as a *law*, such as, for example, the law of gravity. There is no *law* of evolution. There are, however, evolutionary *hypotheses* and there are *theories* of evolution. These can be grouped according to the various levels of creation: inorganic, organic, human, and spiritual.

Inorganic evolution. Theories of inorganic evolution deal with nonliving things, particularly with the solar system and the stellar universe. It seems to be generally accepted by our theologians, philosophers and scientists that the earth, the sun, the moon, the stars, and other heavenly bodies were not created by God exactly as we have them today. Instead the universe has gone through a long period of gradual development. God created and set in motion the "stuff of the universe" so that it would evolve in accordance with His plan. But the precise way in which this evolution took place is still the riddle of the universe to our scientists.

[1] Many present-day physical scientists are not inclined to make such a clear-cut distinction, especially between *theory* and *law*. However, I am told that the traditional distinction is still acceptable to the biologist in whose province both organic and human evolution fall.

In the past there have been various hypotheses and theories which have had their vogue and then have been discarded. There are also the current theories which now have their day. But our scientists have not yet discovered the law of the universe. However, for one who believes in God there is, in general, no necessary contradiction in accepting any of the current theories on the evolution of the universe, provided God is not ruled out of the picture. A similar observation may be made about any of the contemporary geological teachings about the gradual building up of the earth's crust over tremendously long periods of time.

Current theories on the origin of the universe. According to a Cambridge University astrophysicist, Fred Hoyle,[2] there are "three different theories which attempt to probe these mysteries of time and space and matter." These contemporary theories are referred to as the Explosion Theory, the Expansion-Contraction Theory, and the Steady-State Theory. Professor Hoyle, who is co-sponsor for the last-named theory, describes the rival theories in part as follows:

> According to the Explosion Theory, the universe was born a definite time ago. The state of dispersal caused by the explosion will never cease in this theory. The galaxies [of stars] will continue to move apart from each other until, in the ultimate limit in the future, space will present a uniform, featureless emptiness. All activity inside the galaxies will ultimately cease. The stars will no longer shine. All sources of energy will be exhausted.[3]
>
> According to the Expansion-Contraction Theory, the amount of matter in the universe is finite. Even the volume of space itself is finite, in somewhat the same way as the area of the surface of a sphere is finite. During expansion, all space swells up like an expanding balloon. During contraction space collapses literally to a point.[4]

[2] "When Time Begins," *The Saturday Evening Post,* February 21, 1959, p. 38 ff.

[3] *Ibid.* p. 98.

[4] *Ibid.* p. 98.

> In the Steady-State Theory the clusters of galaxies expand apart, but as they do so new galaxies are born, and at such a rate that their average density in space remains unaltered with time. The individual clusters change and evolve, but the universe itself, viewed on the large scale, does not change . . . for the universe did not have a beginning and it will not have an end. Every cluster of galaxies, every star, every atom, had a beginning, but the universe itself did not.[5]
>
> These, then, are the dominant hypotheses concerning the structure of the universe. The decision among them rests with observation. As an example, it would be of great interest to know whether new galaxies are being formed at the present time. If new galaxies are being formed, the Explosion Theory and the Expansion-Contraction Theory would be suspect because they do not provide for such creation. If new galaxies are not being formed, the Steady-State Theory becomes untenable.[6]

To the casual reader, even a popular description of these theories, by reason of the distances and the time and the other conceptions involved, seems almost too fantastic to believe. It is to be noted that Professor Hoyle apparently uses the terms theory and hypothesis interchangeably. Also, his own Steady-State Theory seems to be a species of pantheism in which the universe, as a sort of container without beginning or end, is equated with God.

Organic evolution. In the area of organic evolution a believer in God is free to accept any theory that holds that present-day plants, birds, beasts and all forms of life lower than man have evolved through the operation of natural forces out of one or a few primordial forms, if he thinks the scientific evidence warrants this. He would even be free to believe—although present scientific evidence completely disproves it—that sub-human life itself originated out of dead matter through some form of spontaneous generation. Such theories neither dispense with the necessity of God, the Creator, nor

[5] *Ibid.* p. 99.
[6] *Ibid.* p. 100.

detract from His wisdom and omnipotence. On the contrary, such theories pay greater tribute to the wisdom and omnipotence of the Creator. The man who could design an automobile that would build itself from the raw materials and thereafter replace worn parts and repair broken parts would be far more worthy of our admiration and praise than all the present tycoons and mechanical wizards of the automotive industry taken together. There is no necessary conflict between belief in God and acceptance of any of the current theories of organic evolution.

Human Evolution

In dealing with the question of human evolution it is advisable to break it up into three distinct problems: the evolution of the body, the evolution of human reasoning power, the evolution of the soul.

Evolution of the body. For the theory of the evolution of the human body there is far less agreement among scientists and considerably less evidence to bolster up such a theory than there is for the inorganic and organic theories of evolution. For example, some biologists consider the evolution of the human body merely as a working hypothesis, others look upon it as a probable theory but far from scientifically demonstrated, still others look upon the theory as demonstrated. The theory of the evolution of the human body postulates that

> in the far distant past, perhaps hundreds of thousands of years ago, there lived beings whose descendants gradually changed and diverged along different lines of physical development, some branches evolving into the anthropoid types that exist today, one branch evolving into man. Man would thus not be a descendant of any living ape or "monkey," but only a very distant cousin—not a first or second or third cousin, not even a thousandth cousin, but perhaps a five-hundred thousandth or millionth cousin. What these early hypothetical common ancestors looked like, what too may have been the exact lines of descent, the missing links, and the factors and

processes by which the evolution may have taken place, are all questions on which science offers vague or contradictory answers or no answers at all.[7]

In apologetics (or even from the standpoint of religion) we are not interested in the details of this controversy or in the scientific evidence pro and con. In such a theory of human evolution there seems to be no contradiction[8] to the apologetic proof of the existence of a Supreme Being as the Creator of the universe and all that is contained therein.

Evolution of the reasoning power. There is little or no evidence to support any contention that there has been evolution in human reasoning power. Evidence for such evolution which has been assumed in the past has lessened or weakened under further investigation. Here again, unless the spiritual and immortal soul of man is involved, there is no conflict with a belief in God or religion.

Evolution of the soul. There are no theories which claim to include the evolution of man's spiritual and immortal soul. Such a theory, if ever put forward, would hardly be acceptable to the believer in God. Religion holds that man's soul owes its origin to the direct creative action of God. Since the soul is a simple substance, entirely devoid of parts, it is not possible for it to evolve.

Predestination

Sometimes people are troubled by the seeming contradiction between two known facts, namely, our consciousness that our will is free and the knowledge that God, by His very

[7] Cooper, John M., *Religion Outlines for Colleges,* Course II (The Catholic Education Press, 1947, pp. 28, 29).

[8] From a Christian and Catholic point of view such a theory of human evolution would be acceptable only if descent of the race from a *single pair* and divine causality in preparing those bodies for the infusion of the soul are safeguarded. Otherwise there would be conflict with the doctrines of original sin and of redemption, and with the moral conception of the brotherhood of man.

nature, must know all things, not only our most secret thoughts and actions in the present but even what will be our thoughts and actions in the future. This is usually known as the problem of predestination. Thus God must know when and how we shall die and whether or not we shall attain eternal salvation. At the same time we are taught that we have free will, that we have it within our power to exercise control over our thoughts and actions and to attain or to lose our eternal salvation. We are convinced that we have this free will because our daily experience testifies that this is so.

However, if God knows from all eternity what I am going to do today, tomorrow or at any time in the future, even before I have made my own free choice, do I, in fact, have a free choice? If God knows already what I am going to do, what need is there to do anything, because what God knows I will do, shall come to pass anyway, otherwise God's foreknowledge would be in error?

This apparent dilemma can be satisfactorily resolved if we will try to understand that with God time is always present; there is no past or future. With us time is ever fleeting; only the present moment is ours—the past is gone irretrievably and the future we do not have and may never have. Our vantage point is quite limited, like that of a traveler on foot in the valley, slowly plodding his way along the winding road. The traveler sees only what is immediately around him. He does not know, for instance, that a rockslide now taking place a mile beyond the next bend in the road will effectively block his path and cause him to retrace his steps. But high in a watchtower on the mountain, a forest ranger with powerful binoculars takes in all this at a glance. He sees the plodding stranger and the rockslide which will effectively block his path and make it necessary for him to retrace his steps. The forest ranger's foreknowledge of what is going to happen to the traveler in the valley in no way determines what is going to happen or interferes with the free will of the traveler. In other words foreknowledge of a happening is not the same as determination of or responsibility for what happens.

In this "parable" the traveler on foot in the valley is man, who has been endowed by his Creator with intelligence and free will. The forest ranger in his watchtower is the all-knowing and all-seeing God. His vantage point is infinitely superior to man's. All is present before Him. At a single glance God sees man with all that is behind and in front of him. God knows what will happen to man even before it happens, but this foreknowledge in no way interferes with the free acts of man.

The Problem of Evil [9]

The fact of evil in the world leads some to deny the providence of God or to doubt or deny His very existence. They have heard it said that God is intelligent, good, and just; that He could not be otherwise and still be God. Therefore, everything that He does must always be wise, good, and just. Yet when they look about them, they see much apparently needless suffering in the world and a vast amount of pain, disease, calamity, destruction, and sudden death which do not seem to serve any good purpose. Above all, they feel that if God is infinitely good and just and merciful He should only bestow these ill fortunes on those who deserve punishments. But frequently it seems to happen that the good and innocent suffer while the evil prosper. This, they feel, cannot be reconciled with the existence of a God of goodness, justice, and mercy.

We cannot deny that there is evil in the world without closing our eyes to everyday experience. How then, can we reconcile the existence of evil with the providence, goodness, and justice of God? Although we cannot read the mind of God or act as His counselor we can solve this problem at least

[9] This discussion is based entirely on the use of reason. Revelation, particularly as found in the teachings of Christ, throws clearer light on the necessity of suffering.

to the extent of seeing that the presence of evil in the world is not opposed to the goodness of God.

Much of the evil and suffering in the world can be traced to man's disregard for the moral law, which is known as sin. Thus divorce, birth control, abortion, murder, theft and a thousand other such crimes are violations of the moral law for which only man is to blame. God can in no way be held responsible for these evils. When God gave man free will, He also gave him an intellect to know how to use that free will. If man fails to use his God-given intelligence and misuses his free will to sin against God's law, it is man alone who must be held responsible. God will not revoke or overrule the free will He gave to man, even in the presence of willful sin. In such a case God merely permits the sin—He is not responsible for it. It is man who is to be held entirely responsible for his sin.

There are other evils in the world besides moral evils, such as earthquakes, cyclones, tornadoes, pain, sickness, and the like. These are physical evils, apparent disorders and imperfections which are to be found everywhere in nature. In some instances man could be responsible, in other instances they are entirely above and beyond the activity of man. Sometimes the term "act of God" is used to designate these happenings. At the time they may seem to be unrelieved evils because we are not able to see the good they may ultimately produce. We do know that if they are entirely evil, God could not be their author. But if they are happenings that ultimately produce good effects, God could be their author.

Many physical evils are productive of good results sooner or later. Pain is not always an unmixed evil; it frequently can be productive of good. It is nature's warning that there is something wrong with our system. Thus, the pain of an aching tooth gives one ample warning that he has a cavity in the tooth or an abscess which needs attention. Without this pain one might never be aware of the decaying tooth and it might ruin other teeth in the mouth before the infection be discovered. In a somewhat similar way we have reason to believe that earthquakes, cyclones, destructive lightning storms and the like are nature's "safety valves," through which stored up forces are dissipated that otherwise might collect and eventually bring ruin upon the whole world.

Furthermore, if pain, sickness, suffering, sorrow and the like did not exist in the world, what few opportunities there would be for developing the unselfish traits of character and for doing meritorious things in the sight of God and man. Patience, courage, generosity, brotherly love and a host of other virtues which are so important for the individual and the community would be far less frequently exercised in a world free from these evils. In addition, why should we assume that God *must* bestow only happiness and pleasure upon the good and unhappiness and suffering only upon those deserving of punishment? What wise, good parent gives only pleasure and happiness to his child? Such a parent knows the good effect of suffering and hardship and pain on character development and allows them to occur on occasions when he could intervene. Similarly, a God who would gratify all our wishes would deprive us of the exercise of virtues, and of proving our love for Him.

What we have said thus far gives us reason to see that there is a place for sorrow and suffering in the divine economy. We can see reasons why sorrow and suffering are not wholly unmixed evils but we have not fully lifted the veil from the mystery of evil. There are specific occasions when suffering is apparently needless and when evil apparently serves no purpose, but because we do not see the need or we do not know the purpose, it does not follow that there is no reason or purpose in the mind of God.

The mind of God is infinitely great; the mind of man is small and puny by comparison. Would it not be most presumptuous and foolish for even the wisest of men to think that he can understand or know all that is in the mind of God? Certainly we can reason out, as we have done, that God in His providence has a plan for the universe and for all His creatures. But with our limited intellects it is quite impossible for us to know all the details of God's plan.

What reason have we to think, for example, that the evil we see all about us is part of God's original plan? If it were not a part of God's original plan, could it not be that man's sin brought these evils upon himself? If man's sin has brought these evils upon himself, must we not believe that God, who is all good, has permitted these evils for the purpose of bringing about certain beneficial results which are unknown to us?

Because God is infinite and we are finite, it stands to reason that we will not be able to understand all that He decrees for our benefit. Just because we do not know all the plans of God for His visible creation, there is no reason to deny His provident care of the universe. All the evil in the world cannot produce evidence to deny the existence of an all-wise and all-good God. This is one thing about which we can be certain.

REVIEW QUESTIONS

1. Is there more than one specific definition for evolution? Explain.
2. In what sense is the word *evolution* used in apologetics?
3. What has evolution to do with apologetics?
4. Define and distinguish the terms *hypothesis, theory,* and *law.*
5. What are some of the general classifications into which theories or hypotheses of evolution fall?
6. What do you understand by *materialistic* evolution?
7. What do you understand by *inorganic* evolution?
8. What do you understand by *organic* evolution?
9. What do you understand by *human* evolution?
10. Why are there no theories of evolution concerning man's soul?
11. What do you mean by *predestination*?
12. What connection has predestination with apologetics?
13. How is the seeming contradiction between the doctrine of predestination and man's free will resolved?
14. What has the "problem of evil" to do with apologetics?

15 How is the problem of evil resolved, at least insofar as it is used as an argument against the goodness, mercy, and providence of God?

SUGGESTIONS FOR READING

Creation and Evolution, Ulrich A. Hauber. The Paulist Press, 401 West 59th Street, New York 19, N.Y., 1947. 32 pp., 10¢. (The biblical story of creation; the relation of scientific evolution to the Bible, to belief in God and religion. This gives an excellent account of evolution and reconciles true science with a belief in God and religion.)

The Origin of Man, John A. O'Brien. The Paulist Press, 1947. 45 pp., 15¢. (Except for a statement about the Biblical Commission which is added to the pamphlet (p. 27) this is a reprint of the author's "Creation and Evolution" which is Chapter XXVI in the book, *Truths Men Live By.* This pamphlet shows that the truths of religion and the Bible can be harmonized with the truths of science, particularly in regard to evolution. A theory of human evolution does not conflict with biblical teachings provided that the proper interpretation is given to the biblical passages and provided God is not left out of the picture. St. Augustine's teaching on evolution in the fifth century is quite "modern.")

The Church and Modern Science, Cyril Vollert, S.J. New York: America Press, 1951.

Reni photo

The National Shrine of the Immaculate Conception, Washington, D.C., is the largest Catholic church in our country. It is, first of all, a fitting monument to the Mother of God. It is also a tribute to the ability and skill of the architects, builders, artisans and workers who designed, constructed and ornamented this magnificent structure. But especially is it a tribute to the religious devotion and faith of the millions of Catholics in America who have contributed to the cost of its erection.

Chapter 17

Appreciating the Faith

Apologetics Strengthens Appreciation of Faith

YOU HAVE NOW COMPLETED your introduction to apologetics. Actually your course gave you only a brief survey of the apologetic argument. If this has aroused your interest in apologetics it is to be hoped that you will endeavor to expand your knowledge and understanding through further reading and through additional courses, if possible. For you must not think that you are equipped to enter the lists against all comers and meet any and every argument that may be levelled against God and the Church, without further preparation and study.

We trust that you have gained from this study greater assurance of the validity of your Faith and greater confidence in your Church. You have been made acquainted with the method whereby certain fundamental truths of religion are demonstrated by reason alone. You have seen how definitely reason can identify the Catholic Church as Christ's true Church. As we pointed out in the beginning, apologetics ought also to contribute to a deeper appreciation of the Faith.

When one has reasoned through all the laborious steps that lead from the depths of unbelief to the conviction that God exists and that man has a spiritual destiny, he can better appreciate what a wonderful gift is this divine faith which has enabled him to hold these beliefs without wavering. Nay, more, when one understands what a tortuous road must be traveled by the honest seeker after truth before arriving at the door of Christ's Church to beg humbly for admittance, one can appreciate better what a priceless boon it is to have had always the gift of the Catholic Faith.

For how frequently it happens that blessings, privileges and possessions which one has always had are seldom fully appreciated. If these goods are attained only through considerable personal effort and sacrifice, then appreciation is more likely to exist. Or it may be that having once possessed these goods, real appreciation comes only after we have lost them.

The Born Catholic and the Convert

One who has always enjoyed the blessings of liberty frequently lacks the passionate zeal for freedom that might be found behind the "iron curtain." Frequently, robust health is more appreciated by one who has lost good health or else has never possessed it. Also, a parent often is not appreciated fully by a son or daughter until after God has called that parent out of this life.

As with other blessings, privileges and possessions, so with the priceless possession of the Catholic Faith. The Catholic

Faith is God's supreme gift to us. *"No one can come to me unless he is enabled to do so by my Father" (John 6:66).* How frequently does it happen that the "born Catholic," the one who has been brought up in the Faith from birth, lacks that appreciation and zeal for the Faith which is characteristic of the convert to Catholicity!

The distinguished American convert, John L. Stoddard, has brought out this thought very beautifully in the closing paragraph of his spiritual odyssey, *Rebuilding a Lost Faith.*

> Favored are those, who from their childhood up, are nurtured in the Catholic Church, and to whom all her comforts, aids and Sacraments come no less freely than the air and sunshine. Yet I have sometimes wondered whether such favored Catholics ever know the rapture of the homeless waif, to whom the splendors of his father's house are suddenly revealed: the consolation of the mariner, whose storm-tossed vessel finally attains the sheltered port; the gratitude of the lonely wanderer, long lost in cold and darkness, who shares at last, however undeservedly, the warmth and light of God's great spiritual HOME!

Deepening Appreciation of Faith

Faith is a gift not enjoyed by all. For every human being who receives the gift of the Catholic Faith there are about five who are not so fortunate. Although it is true that the convert frequently has a deeper appreciation of the Catholic Faith than many lifelong Catholics, it is not necessary that this be so. In fact, born Catholics should have the advantage in every respect if they use their God-given reason to reflect on the priceless treasure they have in their Catholic Faith.

What is there about the Catholic Church which the convert Stoddard notes so well, which the born Catholic cannot also experience?

"When I am asked," he wrote,

> what I have found within the Catholic Church superior to all that Protestantism gave me, I find that language is inade-

quate to express it. . . . When I reflect upon that Church's long, unbroken continuity extending back to the very days of the Apostles; when I recall her grand, inspiring traditions, her blessed Sacraments, her immemorial language, her changeless creed, her noble ritual, her stately ceremonies, her priceless works of art, her wondrous unity of doctrine, her ancient prayers, her matchless organization, her Apostolic authority, her splendid roll of Saints and Martyrs reaching up like Jacob's ladder, and uniting earth and heaven; when I reflect upon the intercession for us of those Saints and Martyrs, enhanced by the petitions of the Blessed Mother of our Lord; and, last not least, when I consider the abiding presence of the Savior on her altars; I feel that this One, Holy, Apostolic Church has given me certainty for doubt, order for confusion, sunlight for darkness, and substance for shadow.[1]

To stimulate these and similar reflections we can frequently find help in reading the religious experiences of those who, like John L. Stoddard, have obtained the gift of the Catholic Faith only after long years of travail. There is today a considerable library of convert literature in which we can browse with profit. It permits us to stand apart from ourselves and to see the Catholic Faith as the scientist, the doctor, the lawyer, the historian, the statesman, the artist, the writer, the journalist, the churchman have seen that Faith and felt compelled to seek admittance to it no matter what the initial personal sacrifice may have been. It may be that seeing the Faith through the eyes of the literate convert who has attained it the hard way will serve to enkindle in us that lively appreciation of Faith which is necessary if we are going to safeguard and foster the faith that is within us.

The Obligation to Share the Faith

After all, we must have experienced from day to day the advantages and consolations which the Catholic Faith brings, especially in moments of joy or sorrow, or at times of sickness

[1] *Rebuilding a Lost Faith,* pp. 221, 222.

and death. We are actual witnesses of the assistance which the sacraments afford, especially penance and the Holy Eucharist. In the Holy Sacrifice of the Mass we have a complete and satisfying form of worship. Cannot we bear testimony to these experiences and feelings?

Do we not also have many reasons to be proud of our Church? We should be proud of her definite and sure guidance in matters of faith and morals when around us there is so much uncertainty and doubt; proud of her social teachings, which place her in the forefront of all movements for social betterment; proud of her championing every form of human right wherever there is inequity or injustice; proud of her practical love of mankind in her efforts to alleviate every kind of human distress. Can we not make the effort to convey these experiences and feelings to others not of the Faith?

If we have a real appreciation of what a treasure we have in our Catholic Faith, not only will we take every practicable means of safeguarding and increasing our own faith, but we will recognize our obligation to help spread the Faith to those outside the fold of the Catholic Church. This is the apostolate to which we must be committed.

The Apostolate to Non-Catholics

Now how does one go about the work of the apostolate; or to put first things first, how does one prepare for the work of the apostolate?

Dropping the ghetto mentality. In the first place one must divest himself completely of what has been aptly called a "ghetto mentality." One who is content to withdraw into his own religious shell and avoid all contact with "outsiders" is an example of this ghetto mentality. If it arises because one is conscious of his ignorance about his religion and has been too lazy or indifferent to dispel this ignorance, the remedy is clear enough. Remove the ignorance by reading and study! If the ghetto mentality is, in effect, an "inferiority complex" the remedy, although more difficult, is equally clear. Let such timid souls perk up their courage and brush up on their religion! Possibly our forebears could be forgiven if they hesitated to discuss religion for fear of stirring up persecution and jeopardizing the privileges and opportunities which they enjoyed in this country. But their children have no such excuse. Catholicism is no longer a despised religion of "superstition." All too frequently present-day Catholics not only hesitate to take the initiative in discussing religion, but they also shy away from the sincere and honest questions of non-Catholics.

Non-Catholics are frequently puzzled and repelled by Catholic sensitiveness to questions about religion. A non-Catholic attending a Catholic school and sincerely interested in learning about the Catholic Faith once told me that he had given up seeking information from his Catholic companions. He said they seemed to resent any questions about Catholic beliefs and made it very evident to him that they disliked to get into any religious discussion. On several occasions a non-Catholic acquaintance has asked me a question on religion beginning with an introduction something like this: "Do you mind if I ask you a question on religion?" On being assured that I have not the slightest objection, he has, nevertheless, suggested the precaution: "Now, if you do not care to answer my question, or if it is something that is none of my business, just say so, and we will talk about something else." After such an elaborate introduction there has usually followed a very simple question about some Catholic practice, the explanation of which the non-Catholic had often wondered about.

The ability to communicate. To know your subject well is one thing; to be able to communicate your knowledge to another is something else again. An atomic scientist might be the world's leading authority on the production and use of atomic energy, yet be unable to communicate the rudiments of atomic science to a teen-age boy unless he understands the limitations of that boy's mental maturity and can convey to him essential atomic facts in words and examples that such a boy can understand.

Like the atomic scientists, Catholics have a vocabulary all their own. To the average non-Catholic this vocabulary may be strange and unintelligible. For example, to mention only a few among hundreds of instances, words like grace, contrition, Sacrifice of the Mass, Stations of the Cross, missal, novena, litany, rosary, and so on, may be terms completely unfamiliar to a non-Catholic. The Catholic who is endeavoring to discuss religion with a non-Catholic friend must take this into consideration. When talking with a non-Catholic he cannot use the words and expressions he would use so glibly with a Catholic friend. He must be careful to make his explanations clear by using language that can be understood by the one to whom he is talking.

Depending on circumstances, it is sometimes very helpful to follow up an explanation of a Catholic teaching or practice with a suitable magazine article, pamphlet or book. If one does not have at hand pamphlets or books suitable for non-Catholics, one should at least know where to find them. Throughout this text you must have noted that many such pamphlets and books are listed at the end of each chapter.

In recommending books or pamphlets about the Catholic religion, it is important to exercise considerable intelligence and judgment. It should be evident that you must, yourself, be familiar with the *content* of a book or pamphlet if you are going to recommend it to another. You must make your judgment as to its suitability on the content of the work, not merely its title, and its probable appeal to a particular non-Catholic. This probable appeal may be estimated on the basis of the non-Catholic's friendly or unfriendly attitude toward the Church, his actual intelligence level and education, and his religious background or lack of it.

The course in apologetics which you are now completing, meager though it be, should help in this problem of communication, at least to the extent of increasing your confidence in discussing the Church with non-Catholic friends.

The zeal of an apostle. One may know the Faith and one may be able to communicate his knowledge of the Faith, but unless one has the zeal to share the Faith nothing fruitful will happen. There must be a conviction similar to that which prompted a convert professor of history to declare:

> The Faith is not a secret for a few, but glad good news for all the world. And I think that in such times as the present age, when doubt, despair, bewilderment and anarchy seem nearly everywhere to prevail, there is a special obligation on the part of the convert to declare his mind as freely as he can (*Restoration*, by Ross J. S. Hoffman. New York: Sheed & Ward, 1934, from the Preface).

The prospective beneficiaries of the zeal to share the Faith are by no means limited to those with whom one has personal contact. It is Christ's will that the Gospel be preached to all nations so that ultimately there will be "one fold and one shepherd." Accordingly the spiritual mission of the Catholic Church has always been world-wide. Therefore the zealous Catholic cannot confine his efforts to the home front when the conversion of souls to Christ is at stake. Because the mission of the United States has lately become world-wide in protecting western culture and the freedom of man, American Catholics have a twofold reason for assisting the far-flung missionary activities of the Church either through the Society for the Propagation of the Faith or through the religious orders of the Church which are carrying on mission activities in all the non-Christian areas of the globe except where communism now reigns supreme.

The power of example. In addition to what we might designate the "vocal" apostolate to non-Catholics, there is also the "silent" apostolate of example. This silent apostolate is carried on by one who, in his contacts with non-Catholics, is respected for his personal qualities of mind and heart and who sincerely and devotedly lives his Catholic Faith. This is an instance where actions speak louder than words. We rely on two actual experiences to illustrate this power of example.

A midshipman who became a Catholic shortly after entering the Naval Academy related to the writer the story of his conversion. Born of non-Catholic parents, he was brought up as a church-going Protestant. However, early in his teens he gave up church attendance because the "long sermons bored him." As soon as he was old enough he enlisted in the Navy. There he became acquainted with two Catholic young men. The three became good buddies. They went on weekend liberties regularly and had many good times together. But no matter where they might be staying or how late they got to bed Saturday evening, his two Catholic friends were up and off to Mass on Sunday morning. At first my young friend stayed in bed. After this happened a few times, he began to feel ashamed of himself and, although nothing was ever said to him, he started going to Mass with his two buddies.

Some time later, all three of them had the good fortune to be appointed to the Naval Academy, having qualified for admission through the channels open to enlisted men. Upon entering the Naval Academy my young friend gave "Catholic" as his religious preference, began instructions with the Catholic chaplain and was received into the Church.

He tried to tell me what it meant to him to be a Catholic and how happy he was in his new-found Faith. Tears came to his eyes as he told me the great admiration he had for the buddy to whom he had earlier introduced me, whose clean, wholesome life and devout Catholic faith had aroused in him the desire to be a Catholic. With the help of his friend he was increasing his knowledge of the Catholic religion, but he was convinced that this friend was completely unaware of how much influence he had in his conversion because they had never discussed this.

Another instance of the influence of good example came to the attention of the writer at a luncheon of a group of educators. In conversation with a professor of physics from a well-known secular university, it developed that we had in common a mutual acquaintance, a distinguished scientist at the professor's university. Then my luncheon companion told me that he was a recent convert to the Church and that this scientist, with whom we were both acquainted, was actually responsible for his conversion although entirely unaware of this fact. It seems that my luncheon companion did not know the scientist personally. He had merely a speaking acquaintance with him as a faculty colleague but was thoroughly familiar with his scientific attainments. He had great respect for the man's ability and reputation as a scientist. He also understood that this man was a devout Catholic who attended Mass every day. This fact he could not reconcile with the man's scientific eminence, so he began to read up on the Catholic Church chiefly to satisfy his curiosity as to what there was in this Church that could appeal to such a distinguished scientist. His reading finally led him into the Catholic Church.

Across the table was a language professor from a secular girls' college in the same university city. She apparently had followed the conversation with interest. At the end she joined in to say that the Catholic example of the same distinguished scientist had, also unknown to him, been instrumental in her own conversion to the Catholic Faith.

It was certainly a most remarkable coincidence that two such striking instances of the power of one man's good example should come to light at a luncheon table. But happen it did! I have often wondered how many others have been brought to the Faith or have been stimulated in the Faith by the quiet, unassuming example of this distinguished gentleman. Undoubtedly God alone has the complete score card!

Young or old, high school student or college professor, we can all do some labor in the harvest. We can all do something to advance the cause of Christ and to bring nearer the day when there shall be but "one fold and one shepherd."

The political unrest of today and a quickening of interest in religion, together with a more favorable attitude toward the Catholic Church make the time particularly favorable for the intelligent Catholic to become an ardent apologist for his Church. By deep devotion to his Faith and generous loyalty to the Church the Catholic can win men's minds to the acceptance of Catholic truth by showing that clear, logical reasoning justifies every claim of the Catholic Church to be the one, catholic, apostolic Church founded by Jesus Christ.

"The harvest indeed is great." The apostolate to non-Catholics is Christ's will. *"The harvest indeed is great,"* He said, *"but the laborers are few. Pray therefore the Lord of the harvest to send forth laborers into his harvest" (Luke 10:2).* The Church reiterates this plea in her special *Mass for the Spread of the Faith* in the following prayer: "O God, who wills that all men be saved and come to a knowledge of the truth, send, we beseech Thee, workers into Thy harvest and give to them every confidence in speaking Thy word that Thy message may travel quickly and be made plain. And may all peoples know Thee, the only true God, and Jesus Christ Thy Son our Lord whom Thou hast sent."

The apostolate to those not of the Faith is the work of every Catholic, priest, religious, and layman alike. Each one of us can do his part to hasten the day when *"there shall be one fold and one shepherd" (John 10:16).* We ought to blush in saying it, but would that every Catholic had the zeal of a Jehovah's Witness or of a Seventh Day Adventist, yes, even of a dedicated Communist, provided this zeal could be directed to bringing converts into Christ's Church!

Presently in the United States, there is scarcely one convert a year for every thousand Catholics. And yet we are convinced that we have the true Faith of Christ and are members of the true Church which He established!

If each one of the forty million Catholics in the United States would be responsible for only one convert during an entire lifetime, the number of converts presently received yearly into the Church would be increased more than tenfold. Better still, if each one of the forty million Catholics could be responsible for one convert a year, how long, think you, before the ranks of the estimated seventy-five million unchurched in this country would be completely won over! Yet how many Catholics at the end of a lifetime will appear before the judgment seat of God to confess that they have contributed nothing to the harvest of souls!

REVIEW QUESTIONS

1 What can be gained in respect to religion from a study of apologetics?
2 Why should apologetics give one a better appreciation of the Faith?
3 Why is the convert considered to be more zealous as a Catholic than the average "born" Catholic?
4 What program would you suggest for a Catholic who wishes to increase zeal for his religion?
5 What advantage for Catholics can be found in reading "convert literature," that is, the religious experiences of those who in mature life have become Catholics?
6 What is meant by saying that every Catholic has the obligation to share the faith?
7 What is the basis of this obligation to share the faith?
8 What is meant by the "apostolate to non-Catholics"?
9 Do you think there is justification for the non-Catholic feeling that Catholics are unwilling to answer questions or to discuss their religious beliefs? Explain.
10 Can you give one or two examples of religious questions proposed to you by non-Catholics? If you have never encountered such questions, to what do you attribute this?
11 Before recommending a particular book or pamphlet to a non-Catholic, what should one do?
12 Can you give an account of a convert who was led to the Church by the good example of one or more Catholics?
13 In what way has the study of apologetics helped you?

14 What have you gained personally from apologetics?

15 What part of apologetics was most interesting to you? Explain.

16 What part of apologetics was most stimulating to you? Explain.

17 Have you any plan for personal activity in the apostolate to non-Catholics?

(Please respond to the following two questions under the supposition that they have been proposed to you by a non-Catholic friend.)

18 Why are you a Catholic? (Omit any reference to being born into a Catholic home, to being baptized and brought up in the Faith, or to having received from God the gift of the Catholic Faith.)

19 Give five reasons why you highly prize your Catholic Faith.

SUGGESTIONS FOR READING

Appreciation of Faith

"The Church and Non-Catholic Inquirers," *Things Catholics Are Asked About*, Martin J. Scott, S.J. New York: P. J. Kenedy & Sons, 1927, Chapter I, pp. 1–7.

"Faith," *Ibid.*, Chapter II, pp. 7–16.

"Some Catholic Privileges and Compensations," *Rebuilding a Lost Faith*, John L. Stoddard. New York: P. J. Kenedy & Sons, 1924, Chapter XXII, pp. 216–222.

The Apostolate to Non-Catholics

What It Means to be a Çatholic, Appolinaris Baumgartner, O.F.M. Cap. Catholic Information Society, 214 West 31st Street, New York 1, N.Y. 15 pp., 5¢. (A list of thirty-eight duties and responsibilities of an intelligent Catholic.)

Don't Be Afraid of the Catholic Church, D. J. Corrigan, C.SS.R., and D. F. Miller, C.SS.R. Liguorian Pamphlets, Liguori, Missouri, 1958. 31 pp., 10¢. (Discusses prejudice and misrepresentation as regards the Catholic Church and then replies separately to about twenty-five items of misrepresentation or misunderstanding. The final twelve pages are given over to an open letter "to those who fear the Catholic Church.")

How to Get Acquainted with the Catholic Church, D. J. Corrigan, C.SS.R. Liguorian Pamphlets, 1958. 31 pp., 10¢. (About one-third of the pamphlet is used to explain how one goes about seeking instruction in the Catholic religion and how one should conduct himself during the period of instruction. The remainder of the pamphlet is given over to replying to thirty-three difficulties or objections raised by prospective converts. There is also a brief description of the procedure for reception into the Church.)

A Catholic Invitation to One Not of Our Faith, M. X. Frassrand, C.S.P. The Paulist Press, 401 West 59th Street, New York 19, N.Y., 1947. 31 pp., 10¢. (A calm, simply-written statement addressed to a non-Catholic. Suggests that he is probably descended from Catholic forebears and then throws light on how the Church came to be divided. Invites a return to the Catholic Church, suggests possible next steps, recommends suitable literature.)

Faith of Our Fathers, James Cardinal Gibbons. New York: P. J. Kenedy and Sons, 428 pp., paper $1.00, cloth $2.50. (This book has been called very aptly "the convert maker." It was first published in 1876 while the author was serving as a missionary priest. "It substantially embodies the instructions and discourses delivered by him before mixed congregations in Virginia and North Carolina." The book was written chiefly "to bring home the truths of the Catholic Faith to our separated brethren." A long list of converts testify that it has been eminently successful in doing this. The book has appeared in numerous editions, has been translated into many foreign languages, and has sold well over two million copies.)

To One in Search of Truth, Richard Ginder. Catholic Information Society. 15 pp., 5¢. (Some of the advantages of Catholicism.)

Reasons Against Becoming a Catholic, Warren C. Lilly, S.J. Catholic Information Society. 16 pp., 5¢. (Twenty-nine reasons alleged by inquirers convinced of the truth of the Church but trying to rationalize their remaining outside.)

Why Be a Catholic? Warren C. Lilly, S.J. Catholic Information Society. 15 pp., 5¢. (You have a need for religion and the Catholic Church offers you the best, the most successful, and the most efficient religion.)

Is it Difficult to Become a Catholic? D. F. Miller, C.SS.R., Liguorian Pamphlets, 1958. 23 pp., 10¢. (Explains or replies to the real or alleged difficulties that are considered to stand in the way of those wanting to be Catholics.)

Why Some People Do Not Become Catholics, D. F. Miller, C.SS.R., Liguorian Pamphlets, 1957. 23 pp., 10¢. (Six reasons which tend to keep non-Catholics outside the Church. Also a brief statement on the procedure to be followed in seeking to become a Catholic.)

Father Smith Instructs Jackson, John F. Noll and Lester J. Fallon. Huntington, Indiana: Our Sunday Visitor Press, 1947. 230 pp. (A series of fifty-three instructions for prospective converts presented in the form of interesting dialogues. Widely used, more than a half million copies have been sold.)

Why Not Share the Faith? John A. O'Brien, The Paulist Press, 1949. 32 pp., 10¢. (Sub-title: "How you can win converts." The author tells how to do this, and urges that all cooperate to do the job. If all the resources of the Church in this country were properly organized and put to work, we could have one million converts a year. Some examples of what zealous individuals have done.)

Winning Converts, John A. O'Brien. Notre Dame, Indiana: University of Notre Dame Press, 248 pp. A paperback reprint, 35¢. (A symposium in which many writers active in convert work describe methods which have been successful in bringing thousands of souls into the Church.)

Fallible Protestantism and Infallible Catholicism, L. Rumble, M.S.C. Radio Replies Press Society, St. Paul 1, Minnesota. 43 pp., 15¢. (Ninety-eight questions and answers dealing with the important problem of Christian Church unity and the various arguments and conflicting points of view related thereto vis-à-vis the Catholic position.)

The Catholic Approach to Protestantism, George H. Tavard, A.A. New York: Harper & Brothers, 1955, 160 pp. (For the serious reader, a brief but excellent presentation of the whole problem in striving for a united Christian Church. Examines objectively the roots of disunion at the time of the Reformation, describes what has been done since to effect reunion and what is being done at present. Distinguishes Protestant and Catholic ecumenism. Realistically appraises the present task and suggests a program for Catholics.)

The Slavery of Catholicism, Peter Von Essen, O.F.M. Cap. Catholic Information Society. 16 pp., 5¢. (Deals with the misunderstanding of the supposed conflict between Church authority and personal freedom.)

Glossary

abrasion—wearing away of a substance due to friction
abstract idea—a general idea drawn from particular things; it does not exist independently
acquiescence—silent or passive acceptance
affinity, chemical—attractive force between atoms which causes them to enter into and to remain in combination
agnostic—one who denies that we can know anything about God
alluring—attractive; tempting
alternative—one of two choices
amoral—without a sense of moral responsibility
anachronism—something out of step with the times
analogy—a relation of likeness
anarchy—complete political disorder
animate—living
anthropoid—a type of ape which resembles man
apostolate—mission of an apostle
apprehend—to grasp with understanding
aptly—suitably
argumentation—debate; discussion
Arcturus—name of a giant fixed star
Armageddon—the place of the future battle between the powers of good and evil
ascertain—to find out or discover
ascribe—to attribute; to impute; to assign
atheist—one who denies the existence of God
attested—witnessed; proved
Attila—fifth century king of the Huns, known as the "Scourge of God"
attributable—owes origin to

authentic—genuine; real
authoritative—having authority; entitled to obedience or acceptance
bolster—to support; to hold up
boon—benefit; blessing
botched—bungled
breach—breaking or infraction (of a law)
categories—divisions; classifications
causality—the relation of cause and effect
certitude—certainty
chemical affinity—attractive force between atoms
citation—a quotation
coercive—compelling; forcing
compensate—to make up for
compliance—yielding to others
conclusive—decisive; final
conductivity—power to transmit
consecutive—following in regular order
constituents—elements; components
consummation—completion
contemporary—existing at the same time
contingency—dependence on another for existence
corollary—something that naturally follows
credentials—testimonials of approval
critical analysis—careful examination
cumulative—formed by gathering additional parts
cynicism—faultfinding attitude; distrust of the sincerity of others
denouncement—complaint; public accusation
dependability—reliability
dependence—subordination
Deposit of Faith—sum total of revelation as found in Scripture and tradition
devastating—completely destructive
diabolically—fiendishly; devilishly
dictate of reason—a command of conscience
diffusion—a spreading out in all directions
discrepancy—variation between things compared
divinity—nature or essence of God
documentary evidence—written or printed evidence
dominant—uppermost; principal
dynasties—plural for line of kings or rulers of same family
earmark—identification mark

embezzler—one who dishonestly converts the property of others to his own use
empyrean—the highest heaven
enlightened—free from ignorance
envoy—messenger with a mission
equilibrium—a state of balance
esoteric—for the specially initiated; difficult to understand
eternal destiny—everlasting existence in heaven or hell
ex cathedra—(Latin) "from the chair"; with authority (The pope speaks with authority when he speaks "from the chair of Peter.")
expectation—anticipation
explicit—distinctly stated in plain language
expository—serving to explain
flagrant—glaring
foreknowledge—knowledge of an event before it happens
foster—to sustain and promote
galaxies—vast star clusters like the Milky Way
galleon—a sailing vessel of the fifteenth century
genuine—authentic
geological—pertaining to the science of earth history
glibly—easily; smoothly
harmonious—having parts adapted and proportioned to each other
immaterial—not consisting of matter
immemorial—beyond reach of memory
immortal—will not die
impact—forceful contact
impeccable—free from any possibility of fault
imperishable—indestructible
impetuous—vehemently impulsive or hasty
implication—meaning which is understood but not expressed
implicit—understood though not expressed
inadequacy—deficiency
inanimate—not living
incomprehensible—not capable of being understood
inconceivable—unthinkable; incredible
incredulous—skeptical
indestructible—incapable of being destroyed
infallible—incapable of error
infinite—without limits of any kind
ingenuity—cleverness

intangible—not material; cannot be touched
interrelated—mutually connected or related
interrogators—examiners; questioners
intimidate—to frighten; to make fearful
ironically—happening opposite to what might have been expected
irrefutable—cannot be disproved
keystone—the stone that locks an arch in place
legate—an envoy sent with a commission
logical—according to orderly reasoning
make restitution—restore; pay back
materialistic—emphasizing the material to the exclusion of the spiritual
Messias—the Redeemer
motivation—that which moves the will to action
nebula—extensive celestial gaseous matter
nullified—rendered of no value
nurtured—brought up
objective—external to the mind
objectively—impersonally; without prejudice
omnipotence—unlimited power
orientation—sense of relation to
ornithologist—scientist who studies birds
papacy—the system of government of which the pope is the head
paradoxical—seemingly contradictory
phenomenon—an observable fact or event
philosophy—body of principles underlying a given branch of learning
plausible—seemingly true or reasonable, but may not be
postulate—to claim; to require
precedence—priority of importance or rank
pre-eminence—position of prominence
preliminary—introductory
premise—introductory assumption
preoccupation—engagement of mind with something
preposterous—absurd
prerogative—right to exercise a privilege
presumptuous—overbold; proudly overconfident
primordial—first created; primary
prodigious—vast; extraordinary in quantity
profusely—abundantly; liberally
promulgated—made known; published

propositions—statements to be proved
proscription—prohibition; imposed restriction
providence of God—God's loving care of His creatures
pseudo—spurious; sham; phony
rapture—spiritual or emotional ecstasy
rationalize—to find reasons, even though not true, to justify one's actions
reproach—blame; rebuke
research—careful and thorough investigation
retrospect—a looking back on things past
revelation—that which God has made known to man
rudiments—first principles
ruthless—cruel; pitiless
sagacious—far-sighted; shrewd
scientism—the worship of science
scrutinize—to examine closely
secularist—one who rejects any religious influence, faith or worship
self-evident—easy to see or understand without proof
sense knowledge—knowledge obtained through the senses
sensitize—to render sensitive (to light)
simultaneously—at the same time
skeptic—one who doubts
solicitude—concern; care for
stellar universe—the starry heavens
subconsciousness—active mental state not present to consciousness
subjective religion—religion as it exists in the mind or consciousness of the individual
sublime—noble; lofty
submissiveness—meekness; readiness to submit
substantially intact—nothing of importance added or subtracted
substantiate—to confirm; to verify
superhuman—above the human; divine
superstition—an unreasoning attitude of mind based on ignorance, fear, belief in magic, etc.
supplication—humble petition
tangible—capable of being touched or perceived by the senses
technique—method of procedure
topography—description of the earth's surface, showing hills, lakes, cities, etc.
tortuous—twisted
transgress—to break a law

travail—painful effort
ultimately—finally
unerringly—without fail; unfailingly
unique—without like or equal
universality—state of being present everywhere
valid—founded on truth or fact; well-grounded; accomplishing what is claimed or intended
variance—difference; deviation
veneration—reverential respect
vindication—justification; defense
virtually—in effect but not in fact
weak-kneed—lacking will power or resolution
zoologist—scientist who deals with all aspects of animal life

Bibliography

CONVERT LITERATURE

Dark Symphony, Elizabeth Laura Adams. New York: Sheed & Ward, 1942. (The story of a gifted colored girl who had to struggle against prejudice and discrimination in her search for spiritual peace which led her into the Catholic Church.)

Sorrow Built a Bridge, Katherine Burton. New York: Longmans, Green & Co., Inc., 1937. 288 pp. (The biography of the daughter of Nathaniel Hawthorne, convert-foundress of a religious community dedicated to the care of the cancerous poor.)

Rome from Within, Selden P. Delany. Milwaukee: Bruce, 1935. 289 pp. (His views and impressions after five years within the Church.)

Why Rome, Selden P. Delany. New York: Dial Press, 1930. 233 pp. (An interesting account of the reasons which led a prominent New York clergyman to embrace the Catholic Faith.)

A Testimonial to Grace, Avery Dulles. New York: Sheed & Ward, 1946. (A Harvard undergraduate with no religion recounts the factors which led him to the true Faith.)

Thoughts of a Catholic Anatomist, T. Dwight. New York: Longmans, Green & Co., Inc., 1927.

What Other Answer? Dorothy Grant. Milwaukee: Bruce, 1943. (The story of a modern young American woman who overcame a strong personal prejudice against the Catholic Church.)

We Are Now Catholics, edited by Karl Hardt, S.J. Westminster, Md.: The Newman Press, 1959. 67 + 223 pp. (Personal stories of the conversions of four prominent Protestant theologians in Germany. There is also an interesting introductory essay by the translator, Sylvester P. Theisen, on Protestant-Catholic relations in Germany.)

Restoration, Ross J. Hoffman. New York: Sheed & Ward, 1934. 205 pp. (Through history to Catholicism by a convert history professor.)

Slow Dawning, Jane Howes. St. Louis: Herder, 1946. (A mother with a large family, who believed neither in the Church, the Bible, nor Christ, tells the story of her conversion.)

I Believed, Douglas Hyde. New York: Putnam, 1950. (A convinced Communist and one-time editor of the *London Daily Worker* tells of his conversion to the Catholic religion.)

From the Other Side, Betty Jean Jeffries. Milwaukee: Bruce Publishing Co., 1954. 128 pp. (A Smith College graduate brought up as a Presbyterian and quite an anti-Catholic bigot, according to her own admission, tells a number of interesting, chatty anecdotes of incidents that gradually brought her into the Catholic Church.)

Three Ways Home, Sheila Kaye–Smith. New York: Harper Brothers, 1937. (A British novelist entered the Church with her husband, an Anglican clergyman.)

Salve Mater, Frederick Joseph Kinsman. New York: Longmans, Green & Co., Inc., 1920. (An interesting account of the reasons that led an Episcopalian Bishop of Delaware into the Catholic Church.)

Through Hundred Gates, Severin and Stephen Lamping, editors. Milwaukee: Bruce, 1939. (Forty brief accounts by men and women of many countries and many walks of life, describing the paths which led them to the Church.)

The Catholic Church Invites You, James V. Linden, S.J. St. Louis: B. Herder Book Company, 1959. 118 pp. (A book addressed to prospective converts and to non-Catholics generally, pleading the need for Christian unity and pointing out that in entering the Catholic Church Jews are but fulfilling the promise of the Jewish religion, not repudiating it, and Protestants are really returning to the Church of their forefathers.)

Now I See, Arnold Lunn. New York: Sheed & Ward, 1933. 275 pp. (How *reason* compelled an English controversialist to enter the Church of Rome.)

Within That City, Arnold Lunn. New York: Sheed & Ward, 1936. 285 pp. (A sequel to the above.)

Fast by the Road, John Moody. New York: Macmillan Company. 1942. 308 pp. $2.50. (The author, editor of a Wall Street financial journal, became a convert to the Catholic Church around 1930. Shortly thereafter he published the story of his conversion in the autobiography, *The Long Road Home*. The present book, written ten years later, is a sequel to the first and recounts interesting experiences and anecdotes to show that his "life in the Church has not resulted in disappointment and disillusion" as some of his acquaintances seemed to expect.)

The Long Road Home, John Moody. New York: Macmillan, 1933. 263 pp. (An interesting life story of a well-known business man, one of the country's leading financial authorities, giving sidelights on political and financial affairs and his journey from agnosticism to Catholicism.)

The Road to Damascus, John A. O'Brien. New York: Doubleday, 1949. 248 pp. (Fifteen well-known converts tell of their spiritual pilgrimage to the Church.)

Roads to Rome, John A. O'Brien. New York: The Macmillan Company, 1954. 255 pp. (Fourteen converts, noted scholars and writers, tell how they found peace and happiness in the Catholic religion.)

The Way to Emmaus, John A. O'Brien. New York: McGraw-Hill, 1953. 368 pp. (Eighteen converts, most of them former ministers or students for the ministry, tell the story of conversion to the Church.)

Where I Found Christ, John A. O'Brien. New York: Doubleday, 1951. 271 pp. (Fourteen noted intellectuals tell the stories of their conversion to the Catholic Faith.)

Why I Became a Catholic, John A. O'Brien. Notre Dame, Indiana: University of Notre Dame Press, 1958. (This is a paper cover edition of *The Way to Emmaus,* 156 pp., 25¢. Contains the accounts of twelve converts.)

Rebuilding a Lost Faith, John L. Stoddard. New York: P. J. Kenedy & Sons, 1922. 234 pp. (A remarkable book for the educated Catholic, for a non-Catholic who has no roots in Protestantism, or for one whose thoughts tend toward atheism or agnosticism. Stoddard is sharply critical of Protestantism and would probably antagonize a sincere Protestant.)

The Walled Garden, Hugh R. Williamson. New York: Macmillan, 1957. 231 pp. (Son of a Congregational minister, school teacher, drama critic, historian and finally, Anglican minister, Mr. Williamson reports that he has found both freedom and happiness in the Catholic Church.)

SELECTED TEXTS IN APOLOGETICS

Evidences for Our Faith, Joseph H. Cavanaugh, C.S.C. Notre Dame, Indiana: University of Notre Dame Press, Third Edition, 1959. 16 + 256 pp.

Apologetics, Rt. Rev. Msgr. Paul J. Glenn. St. Louis, Missouri: B. Herder Book Co., 1931. 303 pp.

Faith and Reason, Austin G. Schmidt, S.J., and Joseph A. Perkins. Chicago: Loyola University Press, 1946. 300 pp.

Apologetics and Catholic Doctrine, Part I., Most Rev. M. Sheehan, D.D. Dublin: M. H. Gill and Son, Ltd., 1942. 22 + 238 pp.

GENERAL REFERENCES FOR READING

The New Testament, Confraternity of Christian Doctrine Edition. St. Paul, Minnesota: Catechetical Guild Educational Society, 1941, 480 pp. paperback, 50¢. (This edition is particularly adapted for student use because the arrangement of subheadings makes it possible to locate quickly any incident or miracle in the life of Christ. It is also economical for the student because it can be purchased in either hard or soft covers at a reasonable cost.)

The Day Christ Died, Jim Bishop. New York: Harper & Brothers, 1957, 336 pp. (A realistic account of Christ's last day on earth, written in newspaper style by a well-known newspaperman and columnist.)

God, Man and the Universe, edited by Jacques de Bivort de La Saudes. New York: P. J. Kenedy and Sons, 1953, 421 pp. (A symposium by seventeen distinguished scholars, representing theology, philosophy, history and science, which deals in scholarly fashion with many of the topics treated in apologetics.)

The Dead Sea Scrolls and Primitive Christianity, Jean Daniélou, S.J. Baltimore: Helicon Press, 1958, 128 pp. (Discusses the question of the possible contacts of John the Baptist with the Qumran Community of Essenes and also contacts of the early Christian Church with this community, pointing out matters of contrast and things which they had in common. For the serious reader.)

The Dead Sea Scrolls and the Originality of Christ, Geoffrey Graystone, S.M. New York: Sheed & Ward, 1956, 117 pp. (Includes twenty pages of notes and ninety-seven of text. This book is specifically concerned with "the connection of the newly-found documents with the New Testament, or, if you will, the possible relationship of the people or sect who produced these documents with the spread, the organization and tenets of Christianity.")

The Case for Christianity, C. S. Lewis. New York: The Macmillan Company, 1945, 53 pp., $1.00. (The existence of a Moral Law [Human Natural Law] points to a Supreme Being. Christians believe in one Supreme Being. The unreasonableness of atheism, pantheism. The existence of evil no rational objection against God. Dualism—a God of evil and a God of good—doesn't make sense. Explanation of the struggle between good and evil, the devil and his angels. The redemption of mankind by Christ the Son of God. Man must live the Christ-life. The writer, a non-Catholic, makes a convincing "Case for Christianity.")

Miracles, C. S. Lewis. New York: Macmillan Company, 1947. 220 pp.

(A philosophical approach to the question of miracles in everyday language by a non-Catholic writer who is quite orthodox from a Catholic point of view. In arriving at his conclusion that miracles are possible and reasonable he does a good job of puncturing the assumptions of materialism [naturalism].)

Man Does Not Stand Alone, A. Cressy Morrison. New York: Fleming H. Revell Company, 1947, 107 pp., $1.25. (A brief but eloquent testament of a non-Catholic scientist to the existence of a Supreme Intelligence. Surveys the scientific evidence that points to purpose, plan and providence of God in the universe.)

This is the Faith, Francis J. Ripley. St. Paul, Minnesota: Catechetical Guild Educational Society, 1954, 416 pp., 50¢. (Chapters I, II, III, IV, XIII, XV, XVII, XVIII, XIX.)

God and Myself, Martin J. Scott, S.J. New York: P. J. Kenedy and Sons, 1917, 182 pp., paper, $1.00. (Part I, comprising two-thirds of this book, "An Inquiry into the True Religion" presents the apologetic argument in simple language.)

Man and Matter, F. Sherwood Taylor. London: Chapman & Hall, 1951, 238 pp. (The author, a scientist and convert from materialism at 44, tells of his own conversion in the first chapter and makes a plea for the lay apostolate in the final chapter. In the other chapters he discusses various topics, such as "Biology and Man," "Evolution and Religion," "The Church and Science," etc.)

Index

A NOTE ON THE TYPE
IN WHICH THIS BOOK WAS SET

This book is set in Caledonia, a Linotype face created in 1939 by W. A. Dwiggins, which is by far one of the best book types created in the last 50 years. It has a simple, hard-working, feet-on-the-ground quality and can be classed as a modern type face with excellent color and good readability. The designer claims Caledonia was created by putting a little of each of Scotch Roman, Bulmer, Baskerville and Bodoni together and producing a lively, crisp-like book type. This book was composed by Progressive Typographers, Inc., York, Pa., printed by the Wickersham Printing Company, of Lancaster, Pa., and bound by Moore and Company of Baltimore. The typography and design of this book are by Howard N. King.